FRIENDS IN HIGH PLACES

BY
THE CAIRNGORM MOUNTAIN RESCUE TEAM

D1437623

Cairngorm Mountain Rescue Team

Friends In High Places: (The Cairngorm Mountain Rescue Team,1963-1988).

1. Scotland. Cairngorms. Mountain rescue. Organisations.
   Cairngorm Mountain Rescue Team, to 1988.

1. Title. 11. Cliff, Peter. *1943-*

363.1'4

ISBN 0-904405-54-0

Front cover photograph: *James Grossett climbing on Belhaven (Grade 4),* Coire an t-Sneachda. Photo: *Peter Cliff.*
Back cover photograph: R.A.F. Sea King helicopter during winching exercise on Cummingston sea cliffs. Photo: *John Lyall.*

Printed by Bookmag, Henderson Road, Inverness.

CONTENTS

ACKNOWLEDGEMENTS

Specific thanks are due to: Maggie Barclay for typing the text, Denise Barley and Peter Grant for proof reading, Rob Liggat for making the illustration of the early badge, to Ken Vickers for literary advice and to Stewart Potter for photographic advice.

Past and present team members have contributed text and photographs, and individual acknowledgements appear as appropriate.

Mr H.C. MacMillan, Chief Constable of Northern Constabulary, kindly agreed to write the Foreword.

We are particularly grateful to our three sponsors (The Cairngorm Chairlift Company, The Bank of Scotland, and Stakis Hotels and Inns Ltd.) without whose assistance this book would not have been produced.

FOREWORD

It is a privilege and a pleasure for me to write this foreword, and I know this book will surely provide its own recommendation to all those who have ever taken to the hills in the area of the Cairngorms. Our mountains provide some of the finest forms of recreation this country has to offer. They are exhilarating, stimulating, challenging but, unfortunately, on occasions, fraught with danger.

In 1963 the former Chief Constable of the then Inverness County Constabulary wrote in his annual report: "I am pleased to inform you that only one fatal accident occurred in the mountains of our county this year, which is the lowest figure recorded since 1950". In the twenty-five years which have elapsed since that comment was made the trend in fatalities and serious accidents has been, sadly, ever upwards. One can only speculate, however, as to what the loss of life would have been were it not for the groups of volunteers made up of shepherds, gamekeepers and civilians from all walks of life who, with the common love of their mountains and a deep concern for the welfare of their fellow man, bonded together to form voluntary but organised units dedicated to give aid, so far as it lay in their power, to anyone who found themselves in distress on the hills.

In Scotland, in accordance with the constitutional laws of the country, mountain search and rescue organisation is officially the responsibility of the Police. In this organisation the Police are indebted to the various mountain search and rescue teams, without whom their task would be extremely difficult or well nigh impossible. This book is the story of one such team and is a fitting tribute to those valiant men and women, past and present, who frequently and without consideration for their own safety go to the assistance of others in all weather conditions. If all young, and not so young, climbers, skiers or hillwalkers were to read this book and learn from the experiences depicted herein, I am sure we could look forward to a fall in the graph of fatalities which has signified so much human grief over the past twenty-five years. To go on to the mountains ill-clad or without careful planning and thereby be the cause of an accident which could have been avoided is not only foolish but shows a total lack of consideration for others.

This collection of experiences is therefore most timely and I would recommend this book to all who may have cause to seek "Friends in High Places".

H.C. MacMillan Chief Constable   Inverness 1988

INTRODUCTION

This book is mainly written for the benefit of past, present and future Team members to celebrate the first twenty-five years of the Team's existence. We wished to record the early history of the Team and some of the more memorable rescues in which it has been involved before those early memories and records were lost for ever. It was put to us that other people would be interested, so we ran off some extra copies and have made it available to the general public. This book, therefore, has two objectives: to record the main historical events and to be of general interest.

A rescue team is a very close-knit group and many of the incidents, while important in one way or another to ourselves, would be without interest to others; and so we have tried to keep these stories to an absolute minimum.

What happened as we researched the book was that old files and photographs were dug out of dusty corners, and old memories were dug out of others. It was soon apparent that we had more material than we could ever use, and so we have had to discard some and shorten others, in an attempt to present the main events of the first twenty-five years of the Cairngorm Mountain Rescue Team.

Peter Cliff, Editor. August 1988

Chapter One

PRE 1963

Glen Einich was the first climbing area to be opened up in the Cairngorms, with many of the early lines being worked out at the S.M.C Meet of Easter 1902. There then seems to have been relatively little activity until the 1930's when the Northern Corries of Cairngorm became popular, and this continued through the 1940's and 1950's to the 1960's. But of course there were nothing like the numbers of climbers, hillwalkers and skiers that there are now.

When there were mountaineering accidents it fell on the local police constable to do something about it. In the early Sixties Fred Crayk was in sole charge of Aviemore Police Station. He worked and lived there, and he had to organise searches using anyone who was available — shepherds, gamekeepers, forestry workers, maybe the odd hillwalker scoured from the campsite or youth hostel. It was not always easy for these men to be released from their work, and while many were competent hill men, the capabilities of other volunteers were unknown. There were no formal arrangements for dealing with such accidents, and often the R.A.F. was called in to help. This normally came in the form of the Kinloss Team, a well trained and organised team with professional leaders.

A book published in the 1940's states that the avalanche is an Alpine phenomenon and is almost unheard of in Scotland. Today we know that is not the case, but in the 1940's there were fewer people around to trigger the windslabs or to witness the wet snow avalanches at Easter time.

Here is an account of an early avalanche accident, followed by another story from the early days of Cairngorm mountaineering.

THE LOSS OF GAICK

The earliest people going about the hills were the shepherds and keepers employed in the area, and the sportsmen themselves. The New Statistical of 1835 gives a report by an eye witness of "The Loss of Gaick".

"On Monday 1st January 1800 a gentleman who resided in the parish, Captain Macpherson, accompanied by four attendants went a-stalking to kill some game for a Christmas feast. They intended to return the

1

following Friday. They were to lodge in a house, a good substantial building of stone, which stood on rising ground facing N.W. at the foot of one of those lofty mountains surrounding the valley.

The first two days were calm and frosty. On Wednesday evening came a dreadful storm of wind and drifting snow from the S.E., which increased throughout the night to a hurricane and continued until the forenoon of Friday. No fears were entertained until their non-appearance on the Friday evening. A messenger was despatched on Saturday morning to discover the cause of their delay who on coming near where the house had stood, found its site covered with an immense depth of snow. This induced a strong dread that Captain Macpherson and his companions had all perished.

Upon the messenger's return in the evening a party of twelve men collected and set off early on the Sabbath Morning. The stones which had formed the walls, along with the wood and divots of the roof were seen among the snow, two to three hundred yards from the house. The large stone lintel of the door lay 150 yards distant. After a diligent and fatiguing search of at least six hours the site of the house was found under at least six feet of snow. Only a part of the back wall, one foot high, remained. Four of the bodies were found within the area of the building. Two guns were found on the floor, one bent and the other broken. The other body was not found until two or three months thereafter, lying 200 yards distant and partly undressed. The common people referred to the calamity as a supernatural agency, but an avalanche seems to account for all the circumstances.

The rubbish of the house, as well as the body last found, lay in the direction of the valley below, clearly indicating that the force which destroyed them came from the direction of the top of the hill. It is known that the wind blew with terrific violence in this direction also. The event excited a deep interest in all classes."

THE TRAGEDY OF BAIRD AND BARRIE
January 1928

This account is condensed from a pamphlet, author unknown, written about 1950; and is compiled by Ann Wakeling (Team member since 1977).

Baird and Barrie arrived in Aviemore on Wednesday, 28th December 1927, with the intention of spending a few days climbing in the Cairngorms. After making some purchases in the village they found lodging with Mr and Mrs MacKenzie, at Whitewell. They intended to go to

If it's service you want... come and bank with us.

BANK OF SCOTLAND
A FRIEND FOR LIFE

Corrour Bothy for a few days and go climbing from there. They were strongly advised not to go, as the weather was stormy and likely to continue so.

On Thursday 29th they set out from Whitewell along the Lairig Ghru to Corrour. Some kit was left behind and Mrs MacKenzie doubted whether they had sufficient food with them. From Baird's diary it is known they ascended Devil's Point on the 30th, and that Baird's boots were frozen so hard he had to sit on them for half an hour to thaw the leather before he could put them on.

1st January, Corrour. It is not known when Baird and Barrie left Corrour, but it seems they took a route for home via Cairn Toul and the plateau of Braeriach for Gleann Einich. The writer of the pamphlet, on his way up Gleann Einich that morning, records a clear sky at daybreak but storm raging by 10am, and continuing until midnight.

2nd January, Gleann Einich. A group of climbers had been staying in the lower bothy. They walked home in the morning and met Alastair Cram and his companion M'Connachie going up the glen. A short distance beyond the bothy these two came upon a man lying in the snow, unconscious. They carried him to the bothy, where he died. Cram went to Coylumbridge to phone Dr Balfour, who set off at once by car. Owing to snow conditions he had to return and get a horse and sleigh to get up the glen to recover Baird's body. Sixty searchers gathered in Gleann Einich, but Barrie was not found.

On 24th March, John MacKenzie, head stalker in Rothiemurchus found two rucksacks in Coire Bogha Cloiche, on Braeriach, and this prompted a renewed search with six men from Nethybridge and five from Aviemore. Barrie was found 400 yards from the top bothy. He is buried at Whitewell, where there is a large cairn with the Glasgow Officer Training Corps Coat of Arms and an inscription which includes the following line taken from a poem written by Barrie called 'When I am Dead', contributed to the Glasgow University Magazine at the end of his last summer term:

"Find me a windswept boulder for a bier".

Chapter Two

1963-71

By Ann Wakeling (Team Member since 1977) and Helen Ross (Team member since 1986).

A Team Is Formed

"CAIRNGORM MOUNTAIN RESCUE TEAM READY TO RISE TO THE HEIGHTS" read the "Press and Journal" headline on 4th April 1964.

On Wednesday 1st April 1964 the first Annual General Meeting of the Team was held in the Public Hall, Aviemore, and the Office Bearers, Committee Members and 30 Team Members could feel justifiably proud of the Press acknowledgement. At this meeting the Chairman, Dr T.W. Palmer, reported that: (1) £1000 had been raised to support financial requirements; (2) 23 Team members had attained Red Cross First Aid Certificates; (3) Tommy Paul and Jack Thomson had been appointed instructors; (4) permission had been granted to use the Aviemore Police Station as a base; (5) two Team members (Tommy Paul and Alistair McCook) had been on a survival course in Norway; (6) a Social Club had been formed; and (7) the Team had been affiliated to the Mountain Rescue Committee of Scotland. It was further reported by Police Constable Fred Crayk that the Team had been called out on four occasions. Scotland's fifth official Mountain Rescue Team was one year old.

This gives scant account of the hard work and dedication put into the initial concept and subsequent formation of the Team, so in the best parlance, let's begin at the beginning!

Fred Crayk was, in the early Sixties, the Police Constable in sole charge of Aviemore Police Station where he worked and lived. The increased popularity of hillwalking and skiing had introduced a greater number of people to the mountains, in particular to the Cairngorms with their excellent snow holding properties. In 1962 the tourist boom was well under way in the Aviemore area with the ski road and chairlift attracting hundreds of people every month. There was a consequent increase in the number of accidents reported to Aviemore Police Station: in 1960 — 5 accidents; 1961 — 6; 1962 — 12, including 4 fatalities. There were the fine services of R.A.F. Kinloss to be used in such emergencies but they were not always available. Alistair McCook, a founder member, recalls: "There were so many accidents the Police had to go round searching for

5

helpers". It was obvious to Fred Crayk and a number of discerning members of the community that, if Aviemore was actively encouraging visitors, more practical facilities were required to cope with those getting into difficulty on the hill. In other words, a formal Mountain Rescue Team was required. He approached his Headquarters to this effect. Appended to his report was a list, running to a couple of pages, outlining the "essential equipment and clothing for six men". The paraphernalia a mountaineer takes on the hill, especially in winter, can seem bewilderingly complex to a non-hillgoer, so Fred's list probably smacked of over indulgence to the 'Powers that be'. Nevertheless, the proposal to form a Mountain Rescue Team was approved.

Soon after, Fred had a special delivery! "You've had visitors," his wife said, "look in your office". At last! His 'essential equipment and clothing for six men'. Bursting with anticipation Fred threw open his office door. Total disbelief. There reposing at his desk were six beautifully carved shepherd's crooks! Using the utmost diplomacy Fred conveyed his feelings to Headquarters, and the crooks (appropriate for a Police Station) were spirited away, their ultimate fate being unknown.

Letters, meetings, more letters, invitations, until on the 14th February 1963 the Inaugural Meeting of the Cairngorm Mountain Rescue Committee, convened by Col. J.P. Grant, Younger of Rothiemurchus, was held in the Cairngorm Hotel, Aviemore. In the Chair was Dr J.M. Brewster, Local Area Organiser of the Mountain Rescue Committee of Scotland. Over 60 people attended. A Committee to administer the Team was formed: Chairman, Dr T.W. Palmer; Secretary, Mrs Audrey Mackenzie; Treasurer, Mr Sandy Lindsay. Members: Col. J.P. Grant, Mr A. Dods (Lynwilg Hotel), Constable Crayk, Mr A. MacDonald (Nature Conservancy Warden), Capt Bull (SYHA Loch Morlich), Mr R Clyde (Cairngorm Winter Sports Development Board), Mr L. Carver (Warden, Glenmore Lodge), Dr D. Grant (Forestry Commission), Mr T. Paul, Mr J. Thomson, Mr W. Mackenzie.

Jack Thomson, Colin Gair and Pat Thomas, all founder members, have dug into their memories of those early days. Jack: "After the meeting we took names; Tommy Paul and I were, I think, the only people with real knowledge and experience. They wanted me to take charge, but Glenmore Lodge in those days was really a full time job — you were lucky if you got one day off. Tommy Paul didn't want to be Team Leader either, because he was working for the Chairlift Company which was expanding; but he agreed he would be more or less in charge until we could get somebody trained up well enough from the volunteers. They were young and fit and there was a chance they would be well trained eventually".

Colin Gair: "The majority of the team were in their late teens. Sandy

Shaw and I were both clerks at Grantown Railway Station. The Station Master would only let one go on a call-out and the other had to stay at work. Most locals had never been east of Cairngorm, hadn't seen Loch Avon until they joined the Team."

Pat Thomas: "At the start, as far as I remember, it was nearly all local lads, just ordinary working chaps, they weren't mountaineers or skiers even. Local guys prepared to give up a bit of time. It wasn't as technical as it's got now. Apart from Tommy Paul, Jack Thomson and Peter Bruce who were pretty good on the mountain, the rest of the boys were just ordinary working chaps, prepared to go and lift a body off the hill."

The Committee members, with the exception of the Team Leader and instructor, were not active team members. Their aims, which were subsequently included in the Constitution were: ". . . to foster and support the activities of the Cairngorm Mountain Rescue Team; and, through the Team, to give voluntary aid so far as lies in its power to anyone suffering an accident on the hills and moorlands in the Aviemore District or any other place where the Officers of the Team may direct; to acquire and maintain suitable equipment; to raise funds and administer them for these purposes and to further the cause of mountain rescue in any other way".

Fund raising took many forms. Collecting boxes were put in shops, hotels and other appropriate places in Aviemore and throughout Strathspey. Sandy Lindsay has fond memories of accompanying Archie Dods — "in his Rolls Royce no less" — to empty these boxes. He recalls that the boxes had one inherent fault: they were made of cardboard and the bottoms kept falling out!

Dances were held in the Cairngorm Hotel each Monday night with the proceeds of the door takings going to swell the coffers. In order to identify themselves, each team member wore a Norwegian sweater with a Ptarmigan Badge on it, which entitled them to be admitted free of charge. These dances were highly successful and continued in varying forms for a number of years at different venues.

Letters of appeal were sent through the National Press: "Equipment will have to be provided, the total cost of which is in the region of £25 per man."

There was a proposal to charge for rescue, a minimum of £10 — "to deter foolhardy wandering on the Cairngorms". It soon proved a controversial item. The Mountain Rescue Committee of Scotland pointed out that in no circumstances could any charge be levied for the use of any equipment supplied by the M.R.C. of S. No charges have ever been made, but many of those rescued have given substantial donations.

The first cash intake was used to buy boots and bright red anoraks and

Ptarmigan Badge, copied from original by Rob Liggat.

overtrousers. Gradually were added ice-axes, ropes, karabiners and compasses.

A very comprehensive training programme was drawn up to instruct the recruits in mountaincraft, First Aid, map reading, compass work and stretcher handling. Some sessions were more successful than others — to quote from the Minutes of a Committee Meeting: "Mr Thompson had set a course for the Team, but their first exercise proved that they could not apply the knowledge imparted to them". In other words, they got lost! Founder member, Tommy Paul: "It was great fun when we started — learning and building up the Team. We practised First Aid, map reading and compass work; and we had practical sessions at Craigellachie learning to lower a stretcher down a cliff".

In the early days there was a lack of team transport, with the Police short wheelbase Land Rover being the only official vehicle. It was also the only means of transporting fatalities from Aviemore to the nearest mortuary at Inverness. This could prove an embarrassing situation for the driver and passengers (and an unnerving one for pedestrians hanging around at road junctions or traffic lights) as sometimes it was not possible to completely contain the casualty within the confines of the vehicle. On this same subject, Fred Crayk was most dissatisfied with the arrangements for the storage of bodies awaiting identification. They were held in the garage of the Aviemore Police Station, which was generally in a pretty normal 'garage state' — i.e. dirty and untidy.

A special tribute should be made to the Secretary, Mrs Audrey MacKenzie, who did an enormous amount of work in getting the Team off the ground. To attend Committee meetings she regularly walked 5 miles from her home at Badaguish and back again, often in the dark.

By November 1963 Tommy Paul felt very guilty due to his inability to instruct the team on Sundays because of work demands, and also he had limited time-off to organise the Wednesday evening training sessions. In choosing a Leader 'from the ranks' the Committee gave preference to a bachelor who had transport and a telephone, namely Peter Bruce.

Social at High Range Hotel. Photo by Alistair McCook. Standing L to R: Police Inspector, Andrew Carter, Willie Kerr, Colin Brough, William McPherson, Molly Porter, Jo Porter, Mrs Palmer, Ian Wilson, Hamish Marshall, Alistair McCook. Kneeling L to R: Jimmy Clark, Sandy Shaw, ?, Tommy Mackenzie and Lass, ?, Peter Bruce, Pat Thomas, Charlie Ferguson.

Tommy MacKenzie was appointed Deputy Leader. When Tommy Paul and Alistair McCook came back from their Norwegian survival course in February 1964, the Team was firmly established and was to celebrate its first birthday.

Equipment

One of the first jobs for the new Committee was obtaining equipment. In a letter to Lt Col. J.K. Arthur, Chairman of the Mountain Rescue Committee of Scotland, they asked for the mountain rescue kit then stored at Loch Morlich Youth Hostel to be allocated to the new team. Col. Arthur agreed, and also recommended that they take a MacInnes stretcher developed by Hamish MacInnes of Glencoe.

Tommy Paul reported to the fourth Committee Meeting that he and Jack Thomson had spent a long time looking through catalogues and price lists to choose the best equipment at the right price, but it had not been an easy task because they did not know how much money would be allocated for this purpose. The Committee agreed that the Instructors should be given authority to order goods to the value of £300 for the time being. The Secretary wrote off to various suppliers for quotes for Silva compasses, and also to get a sample boot which retailed at between £5-£6, on an approval basis, and asked them to quote for 20 pairs.

At that time nailed boots were considered more suitable for the Scottish hills but they did not store well; so they decided to order vibram soled boots, and to buy crampons when funds became available. Red anoraks and overtrousers of Grenfell cloth (a close woven windproof cotton) were specially made up by Ellis Brigham.

By August 1963, the stock of personal equipment consisted of: 20 anoraks and 20 pairs overtrousers, 13 pairs boots, 20 ice axes, 20 anklets, 20 karabiners, 20 nylon abseil slings, 4 standard length nylon ropes, one 300 ft nylon rope, 10 Silva compasses, 10 maps, 10 headlamps; and members of the Local British Red Cross were already knitting balaclavas for the Team. Tommy Paul reported to the Committee that the Team was well equipped to go into the hills in all weather, and it was hoped it would prove an incentive for the young men of the district to come forward and join the Team.

But by November the anoraks and overtrousers were not standing up to the rigours of the Cairngorm climate.

Alistair McCook: "They weren't too bad, if they were looked after. They weren't actually waterproof — but certainly a great improvement on what most of us had, ex-army. When we started we all used our own, whatever we had. As money became available equipment was improved, first anoraks, then trousers to match. Most of us used our own rucksacks until there was a general issue of a frameless rucksack with an inner, which pulled out and if you were benighted, acted as a sleeping bag. You could get in it, it wasn't padded, but at least it kept the weather off you".

Jack Thomson complained that another problem in the early days was that there were never enough rockets available on night searches. "We had Verey pistols, but the Police were a bit funny about that — Verey pistols and signal pistols and things that fire cartridges, in mountain rescue. They were used to dealing with guns and people poaching. The Police Sergeant pointed out that what we were doing was entirely wrong — you had to have a licence. I eventually got a letter telling me that I should report to the Police Station with my Verey pistol and my signal pistol, and all my cartridges. Of course I didn't have any, so I went down to the Police Station and I said, "I don't have any". He said, "Have you sold them?". And I said, "No! I never owned them. All I have is the Firearms Certificate so I can fire them. They belong to the Mountain Rescue Team, and they're stored in the Police Station". He was a young constable, a new one. "Is that right?" Thereafter things went a bit easier. I think Sgt McLean took over and got the whole matter sorted out".

When sufficient flares were available the effects could be dramatic. On one incident when it was suspected a man had been blown over a cornice, the Cairngorm Team searched the bottom of the cliffs of Coire an Lochain while members of the Glenmore Lodge Team went round the top. Jack Thomson reminisced: "I was on the end of a rope with two people belaying me. They were big people well briefed by me on what to do if I disappeared. I was walking round the edge of the cornice, in a state of nerves, looking for a hole. I had a massive collection of illuminating flares and I was firing them out over the cornice. As they floated down they looked absolutely beautiful. The Cairngorm Team began firing their flares up, so the whole place was illuminated". The missing people were found safe in the St. Valery hut.

Very early on there were attempts to find, and test, suitable radio equipment. The secretary wrote to the War Office and John Hinde, R.A.F. Mountain Rescue, Kinloss, regarding the best type of 'walkie talkie' apparatus for use on searches. "Ideally the weight should not exceed 6-10 lbs(!). The equipment used by the Hydro Board and Forestry is reputed to be ineffective and always breaking down." Some radios were tested by the Police and a Team representative, and the police bought several sets, to be used by the Police when accompanying search groups on rescues. Team members were not to be allowed to use them. Later, Pye gifted some sets for experimental use, and the repeater station on Cairngorm Summit was built by Pye, and was operational by November '64. This gave a vast improvement in communications; but things still went wrong, as one member wryly recalled — "I was sent out on a search, and I was given a radio from the Lodge which had no battery. I wasn't amused. The person was found safe and well at the Shelter Stone at about 10 or 11am. We had walked in from Tomintoul, and got there at 6pm, not knowing".

Search Party at the Shelter Stone. Photo by Alistair McCook. 2nd left Peter Bruce, 2nd right Molly Porter, end right Sandy Shaw.

Call-out

The earliest call out list so far traced is handwritten and probably dates from early 1964.

T. Paul	Tommy	Boat of Garten
J. Thomson	Jack	Cairngorm House
P. Bruce	Peter	The Hotel, Aviemore
T. Mackenzie	Tommy	Badaguish, Glenmore
C. Ferguson	Charlie	Bridgend, Aviemore
J. Clark	Jimmy	5 Seafield Place, Aviemore
A. Shaw	Sandy	7 Cairngorm Avenue, Aviemore
C. Gair	Colin	2 Railway Terrace, Aviemore
I. Smith	Ian	Dalfaber Farm, Aviemore
A. Millar	Andrew	28 Myrtlefield, Aviemore

P. Mardon	Philip	Reindeer House, Glenmore
C. Brough	Colin	Craig . . . Aviemore
W. Mackenzie	Billy	Railway Cottages, Aviemore
R.J. Fursman	Dick	Boat House, Rothiemurchus
A. Carter	Andrew	The Sheiling, Glenmore
J.A. McCook	Alistair	Woodside, Nethybridge
W. Kerr	Bill	18 Kylintra Cr., Grantown
P. Ferguson	Peter	Springfield, Carrbridge
I. Wilson	Ian	The Glebe, Boat of Garten
Mr & Mrs J. Porter	Molly & Jo	Shieling, Kingussie

Also on the list are the local keepers, to be informed as a courtesy and for information on the best route across their land:

A. McDonald, Conservancy Warden, Loch an Eilean.

J. Duncan, Rothiemurchus.

W. Ironside, Coylumbridge.

And in faded pencil are other names, the 'stand-by' members.

Of the 20 names on the list, only 5 had home telephones, so the Police played a major role in contacting people. They would come round to Alistair McCook's house in Nethybridge, at 1am maybe, and throw small stones at the slates beside the bedroom window in order to waken him. He remembers the small stones being very effective, bumping on every slate as they came down. Colin Gair remembers once being in the Aviemore cinema when the police came in and shouted for any members of the rescue team to attend a call-out. That night he carried the Team lamp — a gas lantern similar to a Tilly lamp with a 14 lb gas canister. There were no headtorches and handheld torches were of very poor quality. Carrying the stretcher out that night was difficult, as the burns were high with melt snow.

In the days before the area got its electronic unmanned exchange, it was not unknown for the news of a call-out to "leak" beyond the callers-out and their appointed charges. There was one incident in which Sandy Lindsay, as caller-out, was asked to go alone to the ski car park where a few other team members were to muster. When he arrived he found he was the first of the team to arrive but not the first person — the local reporter, Jimmy Taylor, had beaten him to it!

"The wettest I ever got" is how Pat Thomas remembers the worst rescue he ever went on. It was at Creag Meaghaidh. A climber fell near the top of the coire. The Lochaber Team had taken him off the cliff when the Cairngorm Team met them and took the stretcher down part of the way. It was a very long carry, so there were many relays. The night was absolutely pitch dark. The headtorches they had gave very poor light and lasted no time at all. They were not on the path half of the time but going through bogs, with a stretcher that seemed to weigh a ton. Pat does not know the distance they carried the casualty that night, but to him it felt like a hundred miles, and he thought they would never see the lights of the Aberarder farmhouse.

Dogs

The Committee discussed dogs and decided to buy an Alsatian puppy for a maximum of £12, and Tommy MacKenzie undertook to train it. Archie MacDonald, a local keeper, was quick to point out that Tommy would be held responsible for keeping the dog under proper control.

Tommy MacKenzie was one of the outstanding characters in the early days. Colin Gair recalls Tommy as the driving force in the Team at that time, most enthusiastic and very skilled in navigation. Jack Thomson says he was a hillwalker of long experience and of such calibre it was unbelievable; he knew the hills so well. If he took a compass out you knew he was in trouble. His was not an ordinary compass from the Mountain Rescue Store, but one which he had acquired during the war from an aeroplane. He carried it in his rucksack, and when he brought it out he would balance it in his hand. He was very reserved, did not speak much, but was a very good hillman.

Tommy attended a dog training course in Glencoe in 1965 and his Alsatian, Lass, gained her 'A' certificate with commendations. Unfortunately she did not have an A1 temper. Pat Thomas: "Tommy's dog was a bit dodgy, like. I think it bit Colin Gair, had a go at him anyway. I can't remember a dog ever finding anybody on any rescue I was on." Colin Gair: "Tommy worked a search dog of sorts, an Alsatian which bit everybody in sight, at which he just laughed. He used to go off on his own with the dog when there was a search. Tommy spent many days searching for a couple whose bodies weren't found for about 3 months." Alistair McCook: "When Tommy got into the Land Rover with the dog, everybody else got out. I DO remember that." Willie MacPherson: "It bit me in the bar one night. It was a dog you couldn't trust, one minute you could put your hand down to it and next it bit you. It went in an avalanche once. We were thinking, that dog's gone. The next minute it came out at the bottom."

There were more dogs later on when others attempted to follow in Tommy MacKenzie's footsteps by training their dogs in search and rescue work. The debut of John MacLean and his Doberman Dot was not auspicious — the dog took off in Coire an Lochain and was not found until 48 hours later! Pat Scarborough had a good Labrador called Tam, and another Team member had a Collie.

Operation Dewdrop 1964, a joint Police/Team exercise to test radio communications. Photo by Alistair McCook. Standing L to R: PC Fred Crayk, Ian Smith, Pat Thomas, PC Murdo McLeod, William MacPherson, Charlie Ferguson, Colin Brough, PC Willie John Fraser, PC Malcolm MacLeod, Peter Bruce, Inspector James Henderson, PC Alan Michael, Bill Kerr, Sgt Duncan MacIntyre, Iain Wilson, Hamish Marshall. Kneeling L to R: Tommy Mackenzie and Lass, Sandy Shaw, Billy Mackenzie, PC Iain Cameron, PC John MacInnes.

Photo by Alistair McCook. L to R: Sandy Shaw, Hamish Marshall, Hugh MacLennan, Iain Wilson.

Chapter Three

THE CAIRNGORM DISASTER 1971

By Kenny Lindsay (Team Member since 1982).

About 1.15 on the afternoon of Saturday, 20th November, 1971, eight young people huddled at the summit of Cairngorm, map and compass in hand, working out a route for a walk to Ben MacDui. Having agreed to head first of all on a bearing of 270 degrees, the party set off. The weather was poor but far from being bad. A low cloud base restricted visibility to 50 yards and a 30 knot westerly wind was blowing snow into their faces. Under foot they found snow about ankle deep and progress down the western flank of Cairngorm and across the col at the head of Coire Raibert was reasonable. The mountaineering club from Ainslie Park School in Edinburgh was heading towards the inhospitable Cairngorm Plateau with the intention of spending the night in Corrour Bothy. Initially, they planned to make for the summit of Ben Macdui via the Cairn on Fiacaill a'Choire Chais, the rim of Coire an t-Sneachda and Lochan Buidhe, before descending into the Lairig Ghru by the Allt Clach nan Taillear. Their leader was 21 year old Cathie Davidson, a third year student at Dunfermline College of Physical Education. With her were six pupils from the school, boys and girls, all aged 15 and 16 and an 18-year-old student teacher. Another group from the club, led by Ben Beattie, had already left and was about 45 minutes in front. The weather had been forecast to deteriorate.

The club had been started the previous year by 23 year old William 'Ben' Beattie, Ainslie Park's outdoor activities leader, a competent and experienced instructor whose drive and enthusiasm had spread rapidly to the pupils. Their monthly meets had included visits to Skye, Glencoe and the Lake district, climbing or walking by day and using bothies for overnight stops. The present walk had been devised by Beattie as a test of his pupils' navigation skills and was intended to push them a little harder than on a normal hillwalk.

After school on Friday the 19th, Beattie, Cathie Davidson and 14 pupils drove to the Edinburgh Corporation Outdoor Centre at Lagganlia, in the shadow of the Cairngorms. Having arrived late in the evening, they could not draw equipment from the Centre stores until the Saturday morning. Then each child was equipped with ice axe, crampons, sleeping bag, survival bag and adequate clothing. General equipment was shared among the party including food, cooking gear, 2 pairs of snow shoes, flares, whistles and torches. The group of 14 was split into a party of 8 fitter and more experienced children and 6 slightly less able.

Both parties would cross the Cairngorm Plateau on the first day and meet at Corrour Bothy for Saturday night. Beattie planned to lead the stronger party himself on a more demanding route, hoping to incorporate the traverse of Cairn Toul and Braeriach on the walk out on the Sunday. Cathie Davidson would lead the second group through the Lairig Ghru for a rendezvous with Beattie at Loch Morlich. As an alternative to the meeting place at Corrour Bothy for the Saturday night, it was decided that, in the event of bad weather, the two groups should head for the Curran Bothy near Lochan Buidhe. Shelagh Sunderland, an 18-year-old student teacher, who was at Lagganlia hoping to become a temporary voluntary instructor there, was allocated to Cathie Davidson's group. Completed route forms were left with the staff at the Centre. The party, in high spirits and now 17 in number, was driven to the Coire Cas car park, below Cairngorm, arriving about 11.15. Following a cold night the Saturday had dawned clear and bright. It appeared to be a good day for hillwalking.

Because of the late start, use was made of the chairlift to try to save a little time. At the top chairlift station, Miss Davidson's group stopped to eat their packed lunches while Beatie's group set off for the summit of Cairngorm. Already the fine morning was deteriorating, but not enough to deter any well equipped, experienced group.

As Beattie's group traversed the col at the head of Coire Raibert, a Venture Scout Unit from Stirlingshire, which had stopped for lunch by the Cairn at the top of Fiacaill a'Choire Chais saw them pass by. The Scout leader, having heard the forecast and observing the threatening weather, abandoned his plan to skirt the rim of the Northern Corries as far as Cairn Lochan, deciding instead to go off Cairngorm by way of Coire an t-Sneachda.

Worsening weather in the early afternoon caused a rapid deterioration of conditions. A strenghtening wind, veering to the south-east, was soon driving snow straight into the childrens' faces. It was hard to tell if the snow was falling or being picked up by the wind. Having traversed most of the upper reaches of Coire Domhain, Beattie's group met unfavourable snow conditions on the uphill western side. Unconsolidated powder snow, often knee deep, made walking particularly arduous and progress slowed considerably. Reduced visibility rendered the landscape feature-less and forced the group to use the method of navigating by one member walking ahead to allow bearings to be taken from him. It was soon apparent that the planned route to Ben Macdui and Corrour was over ambitious and would have to be cut short. Their immediate goal had to be

Curran Bothy — a very small shelter in an exposed situation, at over 3,600 feet on the Plateau near Lochan Buidhe, roughly midway between Cairngorm and Ben Macdui.

Because it was small, the shelter was often snowed over and, in the vastness of the Plateau and adverse weather, could be extremely difficult to locate. After an hour or so of very hard going, this party reached the refuge at 3.15 pm. With 3 miles of difficult walking and treacherous descent into the Lairig Ghru between them and their intended stopping place at Corrour and the weather very bad, Beattie decided to stay put. Nine people crowded into the 12 feet by 8 feet of floor space to settle down for the night. Beattie assumed that, as she had not arrived with her party, Miss Davidson had cut short her walk and made for the St. Valery shelter, on a promontory between Coire Raibert and Coire Domhain, not far off her route. Although that was not a planned bad weather alternative, Beattie knew that Miss Davidson had been there before and it seemed to him a logical detour to make.

However, Miss Davidson's party had ultimately met with extreme hardship. Having traversed the head of Coire Raibert and the rim of Coire an t-Sneachda without any major problems, they found walking becoming increasingly difficult as they crossed Coire Domhain. Soft snow, which would not bear a person's weight, was knee deep, sometimes deeper. The strengthening wind was blowing directly into their faces and it was snowing heavily. Some of the girls were becoming distressed and were crying. Each slow, painful step forward took the children further into the remoteness of the Plateau and further from an escape to the lower ground to the north. Somewhere on this leg the party arguably passed its point of no return — when to retreat would prove as dangerous as going on. As the afternoon dragged on, Miss Davidson, realising that she must head for Curran Bothy to get her children out of the blizzard, decided to follow the Feith Buidhe (the burn which drains Lochan Buidhe to the east) to the Lochan, then make for the Bothy, only a short distance away. But the Feith Buidhe, being in a natural snow accumulation area, was virtually covered over. Only a short section of the burn was found before it disappeared under the snow. With the children tiring rapidly, the onset of darkness and the bothy still some way off, they decided to bivouac before becoming totally exhausted. Efforts to dig a shelter were frustrated as the soft snow simply collapsed and they could not dig into it. With difficulty a semi-circular wall of snow, about 3 feet high, was built and the children huddled behind it in their sleeping bags and polythene bags. By then the weather was vicious, with a raging wind, continuous blizzard and visibility only 2 yards. All that night, Miss Davidson kept leaving her sleeping bag to help the children sweep the snow off them-

18

selves. At first they succeeded but eventually the snow covered the children faster than it could be cleared. Throughout the night they fought continuously against a blizzard which threatened to bury them.

On the Sunday morning, Miss Davidson tried to go for help. Taking the strongest boy with her, she set off towards Cairngorm but the weather was so bad they could not stand and the snow so deep they found progress impossible. After only 25 yards they returned to the party. When they got back they tried to dig out the others, but one boy was completely buried. Two of the girls, in struggling out of the snow, had lost their sleeping bags and were unprotected. An equipment bag was emptied and the girls placed in it; the equipment was soon lost. As Sunday passed, Miss Davidson continually sacrificed the meagre shelter of her sleeping bag to uncover the children but they were becoming increasingly buried and, weakened through her constant efforts, she was unable to cope with the snow.

On the Sunday morning, Beattie, unaware that the second party was less than a third of a mile away, had left the Curran Bothy and made a hazardous descent into the Lairig Ghru down the March Burn. His group then walked out towards Loch Morlich where, about 6.30 pm, they met the principal of Lagganlia. At once it was realised that Miss Davidson was in difficulty and the alarm was raised. An immediate desperate search was organised from Glenmore Lodge with three parties of two instructors going out in atrocious conditions. Two went into Strath Nethy and the others onto the Plateau before going down Coire Raibert and Coire Domhain, heading to the Shelter Stone. The pair in Coire Domhain passed within half a mile of Miss Davidson. So bad was the night that one of the parties failed to find the St. Valery shelter in the blizzard. These searchers soon found themselves fighting for their own survival.

At first light on Monday morning, mountain rescue teams from R.A.F. Kinloss, Police in Speyside and Deeside and the local Cairngorm Team assembled at Glenmore Lodge and were allocated search areas. The Cairngorm Mountain Rescue Team found itself struggling through waist deep snow in an attempt to sweep into the Northern Corries of Cairngorm — Coire an Lochan and Coire an t-Sneachda.

As many of the escape routes from the Plateau as possible were being searched on foot and from the air by an R.A.F Helicopter.

Soon after daylight, Miss Davidson made a last desperate attempt to go for help. She tried to persuade the same boy to accompany her again but he was by then too weak, so she set off alone. Suffering badly from exposure and frostbite, Miss Davidson started out on hands and knees in the direction of Cairngorm.

When she had gone only a few hundred yards she was spotted by a

Glenmore Lodge instructor who was acting as observer aboard an R.A.F. helicopter which had managed to find a break in the cloud and fly over the Plateau. Miss Davidson was immediately picked up and managed only a few words: "Burn — Lochan — buried", but it was enough to indicate where the children were. Thickening cloud and the urgent need to get Miss Davidson to hospital forced the helicopter to pull out and the information gained was passed to Glenmore Lodge. With increased urgency the rescue attempt was concentrated on the Feith Buidhe.

Late in the afternoon, the stricken party was found buried under 4 feet of snow by Ben Beattie and the Principal of Lagganlia. Of the 7 Miss Davidson had left, only one remained alive. A flickering of his eyelids showed Raymond Leslie had survived, completely buried but with an air space round his head. He was evacuated in critical condition by a helicopter approaching from Loch Avon, and flown to hospital in Inverness. Deteriorating weather prevented the removal of the bodies that day and the rescue teams had to leave them on the Plateau. Next day, clearing weather allowed helicopters to fly to the Feith Buidhe and uplift the bodies.

Normally mountain accidents affect only those directly involved but this incident, soon to become known as "The Cairngorm Disaster", aroused great public interest. Every detail was reported by the media. Questions were asked and statements made in the House of Commons. The local MP even called for a "harbourmaster of the hills" with authority to permit or prevent people going to the hills according to the weather conditions, an idea which luckily did not materalise. February of the following year saw a Fatal Accident Inquiry at Banff in which every aspect of the incident was scrutinised. Perhaps the issue which raised most debate was the presence of high level bothies in the Cairngorms — did they attract less able people into remote areas as they offered safety and shelter in adverse weather? These shelters were eventually removed from the Cairngorms. After six days of evidence the jury rejected pleas by counsel to apportion blame, and returned formal verdicts on the deaths of the unfortunate six, while putting forward some reasonable suggestions as to the future safety of children in the hills. No restrictions were called for and it was stated that the jury members had no wish to stifle the spirit of adventure associated with outdoor pursuits. There was no scapegoat and it was concluded that a succession of human errors led to the enormous loss of young lives — a tragedy of such proportions never seen before, or since, on the mountains of this country.

Chapter Four

1971-1981

*By John Allen (Team Member since 1972 and current Deputy Leader)
and Martin Robertson (Team Member 1972-1980 and Chairman
1977-1980)*

Prior to the 1971 disaster the Committee had been considering the
strength of the Team. At a meeting in October 1971 the list of Team
members was reviewed and according to the Minutes it was agreed to
place an advertisement in the local paper inviting potential recruits to
come to a public meeting on 25th November. In the event this meeting
was overtaken by the disaster and it was postponed until later in December, when it was extremely well attended by 70 people. Sergeant Ian Boa
and doctor Neil MacDonald addressed the meeting, a total of 43 names
were taken of those interested in joining and it was decided to start a
training programme straight away.

It was not possible to provide equipment for so many people and the
prospective members therefore had to provide their own. The Committee hoped that a natural selection would occur during the training
sessions. The first outdoor session was on 6th January 1972 when Alistair
McCook led a party to Jean's Hut and Mollie Porter took another group
onto the Cairngorm Plateau. The first indoor navigation lessons were
made possible by the loan of extra maps and compasses from Fred Harper
at Glenmore Lodge.

The training progressed, the Team developed, and on 14th December
1972 Alistair McCook decided that he was then able to stand down as
Team Leader. Mollie Porter, who was Team Secretary, was appointed in
his place with Morton Fraser as Depute. Jack Thomson, Chairman,
thanked Alistair McCook for his work during this difficult period and
Alistair was appointed Honorary President.

By late 1972 fund raising was becoming a major issue. While personal
equipment was a priority, the Team also needed a vehicle. Mollie had
begun writing letters to major British companies with a request for a
donation, and this turned out to be a very worthwhile exercise. A
sub-committee was formed to organise the first Sponsored Walk to the
Shelter Stone and this proved to be an excellent fund raiser and to lay the
foundations for many subsequent walks through the Lairig Ghru. In 1974
Fred Moodie of the Spey Valley Tourist Organisation persuaded the
Grant's Whisky Company to donate a Land Rover to the Team and the

Presentation of Land Rover. 1974. Standing L to R: John Gould, John Dallas, Molly Porter, John King, Jo Porter. Sitting L to R: John Weston, Bruce Reynard.

vehicle was officially presented at the Aviemore Ice Rink in the Autumn of that year. By the mid-1970's the Team was adequately supplied with personal and general equipment, although the renewal and upgrading of equipment continued (and continues) to be a problem.

From her appointment as Team Leader in 1972 the Team's development was greatly influenced by the enthusiasm and energy of Mollie Porter. In her dual roles of Secretary and Leader she devoted much of her time to Team affairs. The result was a much improved and more efficient Team. She resigned in 1980, when the leadership passed to the present Team Leader, Peter Cliff.

A QUICK FLASH

By Gordon Stewart (Team Member since 1986)

False alarms inevitably occur quite often in the Mountain Rescue business. Sometimes these can be rather annoying, but they occasionally bring a touch of hilarity to otherwise routine proceedings. Two similar incidents of this type occurred in 1973.

On the night of February 14th, four members of the Cairngorm Team were called out to investigate flashing lights on Meall a'Bhuachaille, a

2,654 ft hill to the north of Loch Morlich. These had been spotted by climbers who were staying at Jean's Hut in Coire an Lochain. Two experienced mountaineers had recognised the lights as the Alpine distress signal; six flashes followed by a pause, and had carefully taken compass bearings, thus deciding that someone was in distress on the upper slopes of Meall a'Bhuachaille. They felt so sure of this that they took the trouble to walk to the Cairngorm car park to inform the Police.

Conditions were extremely cold, frosty and clear: quite a nice night for a search really. The little group had almost reached the summit of the hill when suddenly someone saw the flashes. Sure enough it was the Alpine distress signal, but it wasn't a walker in danger on Meall a'Bhuachaille. It was a lighthouse on the Cromarty Firth, thirty miles away! A local bobby who was accompanying the Team members was rather upset to discover that their search had been a waste of time and he sent a rather curt radio message back to the Aviemore base. Unfortunately for him radio communications were very good that night due to the clear air, and not only was his message heard in Aviemore, it was also heard in the Police Headquarters in Inverness. Apparently a senior officer reminded him that bad language was not allowed over the air!

On another very fine night in July of the same year some walkers reported having seen flashes in the sky over Cairngorm. It was assumed that these were distress flares and the Cairngorm Team was called out en masse to investigate. No one was very sure exactly where to look for these distressed mountaineers and so the searchers were sent off in pairs to range widely over the Cairngorm area. It was such a beautiful night that it seemed almost impossible that anyone could have become lost, and the reports were so vague that some of the members were rather sceptical about the whole affair.

Anyhow people continued to search the hills and look for further flashes.

Meanwhile at Glenmore Lodge, Fred Harper, Principal of the Lodge, who was co-ordinating operations, had been doing an investigation of his own. At about 2.15 am there was a radio message: "This is Glenmore Base. Message to all teams. I want you all to look into the Eastern sky at 02.27 hrs. I've had a report from the MET office that SKYLAB will then be directly over Cairngorm and proceeding in a westerly direction!".

You may remember that SKYLAB was a satellite that happened to be zooming around at that time. Fred had discovered through his enquiries that the time of its last flight over the area seemed to coincide with the original sighting of the flashes. The searchers sat down and waited. Sure enough, at 2.27 on the dot a mighty flash was seen streaking across the sky. The Cairngorm Mountain Rescue Team went home to bed.

MAYHEM IN THE MARSHES
by Gordon Stewart

Not all rescues involving the Cairngorm Team are in the mountains. In the Summer of 1973 a search was conducted in the Insh Marshes near Kingussie for a missing child. A thirteen year old girl had gone out riding on her pony in the evening but had not returned. Her concerned parents contacted the Police, and the Rescue Team was called out at about 10 pm.

She was known to have been riding on the banks of the Spey, and it was decided to carry out a line search from Kingussie downstream towards Kincraig. At some early point in the proceedings, Lyall Blackwood, one of the Team characters of the time, was seen to have acquired a duck which he concealed in his coat! The search progressed in the darkness through the mud and slime of the Marshes, until around midnight when a wee voice was heard calling for help. The young girl was found safe and well, sitting in a bog near the River. She was quite unconcerned about her own safety, but rather worried about her horse which had scarpered and swum across the Spey as a result of the racket being created by the Rescue Team as they floundered through the difficult ground!

The father was delighted to have his daughter back safely and invited the Team up to his house to partake of sandwiches and a crate of his own brand of malt whisky. He wasn't the least bit bothered about the muddy and dishevelled state of the heroes as he ushered them into the drawing room to sit down in the comfy chairs. Throughout all the searching and imbibing the duck remained safely inside Lyall's coat!

The story had a totally happy ending when the pony was returned safely the next day, and such was the little girl's gratitude to her rescuers that she wrote an individual letter of thanks to each member of the team.

BELGIUM WAS NEVER LIKE THIS
by Gordon Stewart

One incident which seems funny now but probably wasn't funny at the time was the case of the seven Belgians. This rescue occurred on Thursday, 9th September 1976 in the vicinity of Coire Raibert. The group, three girls and four men, all in their twenties, were camping at the Glenmore campsite when they decided to go for an overnight trip to the Shelter Stone. They sensibly attempted to obtain information about the walk, and with this in mind, went along to the Forestry Information Office. Whatever they were told they decided that the trip was on, and they set off in reasonable weather to spend Wednesday night at the well-known howff.

Down by Loch Avon an English outdoor instructor, Chris Watt and his girlfriend Peggy, who were on holiday in the area, were just settling down for a cosy, quiet night when the seven Belgians appeared, asking about the whereabouts of the Shelter Stone. It must have come as a great shock to them to be informed that this grim boulder heap was the very place at which they were destined to spend the night. Apparently they had been expecting a comfortable Alpine-style hut with bunk beds, blankets, heating, cookers and a friendly warden. Instead, to their horror, they discovered that the Shelter Stone was in fact . . . a stone! Having planned their trip with hut accommodation in mind and having no previous experience of Scottish mountain conditions, they were very poorly equipped in terms of clothing, food and equipment. At the time of their arrival they were already wet and tired, and the thought of a miserable hungry night under a rock must have been quite appalling. They had thin sleeping bags, but few dry clothes and no stove or hot food. There was no alternative but to cram themselves into the howff along with Chris and Peggy and, after a snack of hard boiled eggs, bread and jam, attempt to get a night's sleep. Conditions inside were dismal due to overcrowding and dampness and, to make matters worse, the weather outside was developing into a real Cairngorm blizzard with heavy snowfall and 85 knot winds.

In the morning the anxious Belgians sought the assistance of Chris and Peggy to get them out of their predicament. The decision was made to lead the group out by way of Coire Raibert, then across the plateau and into Coire Cas. Before they set off they ate the remainder of their cold food and had a hot drink provided by Chris. Clad in light cotton jeans, Hush Puppies, wellingtons and plimsoles they began an horrendous journey through deep drifting snow and fierce winds. By the time they reached the steep upper section of the Coire three of the group, all male, were showing signs of exposure, one of them severely. Chris decided to leave them there inside sleeping bags, in the shelter of a snow bank, while he concentrated on getting the others down safely.

After an arduous struggle across the plateau and down the Fiacaill of Coire Cas, they managed to reach the car park, exhausted but still on their feet.

Once the alarm was raised help was organised quickly. The Rescue Team was forced to travel on foot since conditions were too bad to permit the use of a helicopter. Thanks to detailed information given by Chris, the rescuers knew what equipment was required and exactly where to locate the casualties. The eighteen members of the rescue party carried the three Belgians out on stretchers and, once back in civilisation, they made a good recovery and were none the worse for their nightmarish ordeal.

Apart from the unusually severe conditions (for September) and the inexperience of the Belgians, the major cause of the mishap was the inadequate information available at that time for people venturing onto the hills. The thought of the hapless group turning up at the Shelter Stone expecting to see an Alpine hut raises a laugh, but at the same time one sympathises with them to the extent that, mature adults as they were, they may never have got into distress had they been given accurate and detailed information about the nature of their expedition. So they were unlucky to find themselves in a dreadful situation that need never have arisen. However they were lucky to encounter Chris Watt, whose prompt and appropriate action perhaps saved the lives of the entire party and averted a major disaster.

TO BENALDER BY BOAT

by Gordon Stewart

My first experience involving the Cairngorm Mountain Rescue Team was in March 1978, when I was staying at Benalder Bothy with a party from Lanark Grammar School. I was in first year at University, but still maintained an interest in my old school hillwalking group. I was aware of the existence of the various Rescue Teams, but in my three years' mountaineering experience I had been lucky enough not to have been involved in any incidents involving casualties or rescues. Consequently I hadn't given the rescue service much thought, apart from the vague notion that the volunteers involved must all be very hardy and heroic! I would never have believed at that time that I would eventually join the Cairngorm Team myself, only to discover that the team members, far from being supermen (or women), were just ordinary punters like myself, recruited from all walks of life.

The incident at Benalder occurred on the 24th March during a spell of typically wild, wintry weather. Our party had been out during the day on Beinn Bheoil in relatively good conditions, but were glad to return to the comfort of the bothy as the weather was turning nasty, with snow and strong winds. Such conditions don't worry the walker when he's safely settled down in front of the bothy fire with a plate of stew and a pint mug of tea. You don't expect anything to intrude on your cosy hard-earned comfort. On this occasion it did. At about 8.30pm when the storm had been raging for a few hours, the door suddenly burst open, a figure stumbled in and a high-pitched Glaswegian voice shouted "Help! There's a wee boy up the track has fell doon. He's nearly deid!".

Whether it was the panic-stricken sound of the young lad's voice or the nature of the message he conveyed, the effect on the relaxed atmosphere of the room was sudden and dramatic. Immediately people were rushing around, grabbing outdoor gear and torches and heading out into the darkness. The boy had collapsed near the bothy and by the time I had reached the door he was already being carried towards the building by teachers from our party. They were experienced hill leaders and knew what had to be done to warm and revive the lad, who was suffering badly from exposure. Two other adults, who had just arrived that same evening, having walked the eight miles from Rannoch, volunteered to walk out again to call the Mountain Rescue.

The casualty was a fourteen year old member of a Boy's Brigade group from Glasgow, who had been walking to Benalder from Corrour Station via the Bealach Chumhainn.

The leaders of the group were older BB lads who had gone on ahead, not realising that one of their party was becoming cold and tired. The severity of the weather was the main cause of the incident, although the situation was certainly made worse by the inexperience of the boys and their inadequate equipment (including lightweight boots, jeans and kit-bags instead of rucksacks).

Having made the casualty as safe and comfortable as possible we all retired to bed to await the arrival of the Rescue Team. At about 5am, I heard a noise which was the arrival of Molly Porter with other team members. One of the teachers went to the door to explain what was what and in the morning the boy was gone. He later made a full recovery in hospital. His friends spent the next day in the bothy, as did our own party because the weather was still foul. The following day we escorted them out to Rannoch and they went off home having learned a useful lesson.

The unusual thing about the rescue operation was that the Team arrived by boat, having made a rough passage of over an hour from Benalder Lodge, across the dark storm-swept waters of Loch Ericht. This was made possible by the generosity and expertise of George Oswald and his assistant from Benalder Estate. This action on the part of the Team and the boatmen undoubtedly speeded the operation and hastened the recovery of the casualty.

HELICOPTER

by Ian Ross (Team Member since 1980)

(1) The car park is empty. Five hours earlier, the weekend revellers in cerise and turquoise laughed, argued, queued, slipped, spilled and skied in the Cairngorm fairground. Now only the empty car park remains, the frozen grimy slush covered with cleansing snow, and the only noise left is the moan of the wind, rising and falling, blowing the snow in mad spirals across the flat, deserted place.

In the corner, by the dark, locked buildings, is a single transit van, battered and swaying with every gust. Inside, six people, outwardly good humoured, but each with private thoughts, are waiting. The radio crackles to life, giving them their instructions; and the door is opened, sending a shower of ice particles over the occupants. Each prepares his equipment, cocooning himself against the unwelcoming environment. They wait again, outside, and listen; but only hear the moan of the wind. A collar is zipped more closely. Listening. A faint rumble. Rhythmic thuds. 'Do you hear it?'. No-one sure. They scan the dark for any movement. Nothing.

Without warning, a bright, dazzling light appears at the end of the car park, not from the sky but seemingly from under the ground. The noise is suddenly louder. A single bright eye, shining in the blackness, appearing from nowhere, rising up from the ground. The noise is getting louder. More lights. Green. Red.

The lights stop rising and move along the car park, not apparently in the air, not like a vehicle on the ground, but between. Floating. There is no shape. Only lights and noise, getting nearer and louder. Everyone is smothered in noise. Snow is driven hard in everyone's faces and all turn their backs on the manifestation. The lights have stopped moving. The snow is blown away, but still the numbing noise remains. The people move as one, on a signal, towards the lights. As they get closer, a yellow shape emerges, then a large door, five feet above the ground, with welcoming, helping hands. Sit down, lap belt on, look round, catch each other's eyes, a roar, the seats sway and bank, the ground falls down below.

The car park is empty, only the moan of the wind and the dancing snow remain.

(2) We were to group in Glen Feshie, where a helicopter was to fly us into the coire. There must have been about eight or ten of us, and one of Denise's Bearded Collie dogs. In we piled as usual, up into the sky, and all seemed normal.

Unfortunately there was low cloud and the pilot could not take us into the main, flat bottomed part of the coire. Coire Garbhlach is unusual, in that the approach is V-shaped with interlocking spurs, and as such offers nowhere to land a helicopter.

By signs and shouting the winchman told us we would have to jump out. I remember thinking 'You must be joking. Jump onto what?!'. Anyway, we did. About six feet, onto the steep scree above the waterfall. As we cowered below the shaking juggernaut, we were showered by falling rucksacks as the winchman dropped them on top of us.

Then the picture I will always remember. Bob the Beardie — flying through the air to land in a heap beside us. He seemed to enjoy it! The chopper was off and we were left to pick up our scattered belongings, including two rucksacks which had fallen over the waterfall.

Team Member being winched into RAF Sea King. Photo by the Sunday Express.

Inside a Sea King. Photo by the Sunday Express.

SEARCH AND RESCUE DOGS

By Denise Barley (Team Member 1977-86)

In 1976 I learned of the existence of the Search and Rescue Dog Association (S.A.R.D.A.) and was immediately hooked on the idea. With the help of Pat Wells, who worked a dog called Tam, I started with a Golden Retriever puppy. I was inexperienced and she wasn't very clever (the puppy, that is — not Pat Wells. Editor), so we didn't make a very good impression on my first S.A.R.D.A. training course in December 1976. I switched to my Bearded Collie, Bess, and everything fell into place. She was very much at home in the mountains, had a keen brain and loved the work. The two of us went onto the S.A.R.D.A. Call-out List for Scotland in December 1977, by which time both my husband Chris and I were also members of the Cairngorm Team.

We went through a lot of hard times together, she and I, and the outer image we presented didn't exactly help — a short suburban female and a hairy pedigree dog are hardly what people imagine mountain rescuers to be made of! The first time the R.A.F. Team was asked to supply me with a companion for a night search of the Lairig Ghru (a lone skier missing on Braeriach) they took one look at me and hauled out their newest recruit. He had more Mars Bars than navigational equipment in his rucsack, and was not best pleased when at 5am, after a night of wading up through the snows of the Lairig and back, I decided to stay in the Sinclair Bothy in order to start a new search area at dawn. He had a sleeping bag and I didn't (very silly of me), but drawing room manners didn't count for much in a Cairngorm snowstorm — he snored the rest of the night away in the comfort of his sleeping bag, while Bess and I huddled in icy discomfort on a soggy wooden bench.

As a S.A.R.D.A. handler you can be called anywhere in Scotland at any time, which makes it a hazardous and demanding occupation. As well as being a decent dog handler you must be very sure of yourself as a mountaineer, able to cope with difficult terrain which you have never seen before, in the middle of the night with the worst weather that Scotland can throw at you. You are usually alone except for your dog. I was sometimes frightened by what I was doing, but a bit of adrenalin helps the concentration! The only time I remember all the S.A.R.D.A. handlers openly discussing how frightened they'd been was when several of us (and several rescue teams) combed Beinn A'Ghlo near Blair Atholl for a missing solo walker. Each dog handler was sent to one of the many corries along the mountain's west flank, and we all spent the day on very unstable snow, in thick mist, alone and out of radio contact with base. We could, however, raise each other on the radio, so messages of comfort were passed back and forth. By this time I was working Charlie, my second Beardie. He wasn't as clever or as dedicated as Bess, so searching with him was much harder work for me, but Bess had arthritis and I didn't want to push her into an early grave. Charlie's worst night was when we turned out in the Cairngorms for climbers last seen stuck on Hell's Lum, across the plateau. My dog had a badly cut paw, so I opted for Coire an-t-Sneachda, while Tony Flood and his labrador Wellie went over the plateau. Dave Craig, Chris (my husband) and I wallowed around in blinding spindrift and deep drifts all night, and were very pleased to be coming out at dawn, when Fred Harper asked us on the radio to go up and over the plateau to help Tony's party, who had found the climbers still at Hell's Lum. That was a hard trip! By the time the whole sorry business was over and we were helping to carry a body back, we had been out eleven hours and Charlie actually had bags under his eyes, poor dog. On the next call-out, to make up for taking the soft option previously, I went up on the plateau while Neil Baxter and his dog Shebe went over to the Lairig Ghru, looking for an overdue couple. He found them down in the Lairig, while I had the pleasure of slithering down a verglassed Goat Track without an ice-axe at 2 o'clock in the morning.

Dogs are often airlifted into search areas, and in 1979 Kenny Macken-zie (Secretary of S.A.R.D.A.) asked me to design a harness suitable for winching a dog into and out of a helicopter. It was to be adjustable to fit different sizes of dog. I based my design on the method used for unloading horses from ships in the First World War — a rectangular piece of fabric to pass under the body, with a strap under the tail and round the chest, and more straps for securing and carrying over the top of the body. That design gradually spread around the country and is now used by many rescue dog handlers, and is, I believe, manufactured commercially. I still have a photograph of my first prototype, with Charlie dangling miserably in it from our loft . . . But then Charlie never did like being winched.

My third dog, Bob, loved helicopters: he used to sit next to the winchman at the open door and look at the view. Bob was in many ways my best dog, but by the time he came along I was changing my interests and losing my fitness, so I was never really good enough to match him. On two occasions he indicated to me that he had found missing people (on his first call-out a little girl drowned in a river, and on his last a young boy lying with a broken leg in a gully on Creag Dubh) and I failed to read him properly, although he did all he could to tell me. He was tremendously strong and hardy in the worst winter weather. The only time I saw him flag was after a long day in very deep snow in Coire Garbhlach, but a little pork pie from John Allen woke him up like Popeye eating spinach.

(Peter Cliff: John Allen has quite a reputation for having particularly

Charlie, Bob and Bess. Photo by Denise Barley.

good lunch boxes. I once proudly produced a similar miniature pork pie, asking John if he had ever seen them. He said, 'Yes, he had; and had I seen these?' — producing a smoked quail in aspic!).

Bob got himself onto television rather a lot, as he was also a successful show dog, winning Best of Breed at Crufts 1985; and this eventually became something of an embarrassment to me, as I felt there were so many dog handlers around the country working just as hard and enduring just as much with their dogs, and yet we seemed to be getting the publicity.

I retired from mountain rescue in 1986, as I was no longer spending enough spare time in the mountains to be confident of coping with everything I might be asked to do. But Graham Clarke and his labrador Sam, and the tireless Police dog handlers of Highland Region, especially Constable Jimmy Simpson of Aviemore Police, are still there, turning out at midnight to search through the night until dawn when the main groups come out.

A CHAIRMAN'S VIEW

By Martin Robertson (Team Member 1972-1980 and Chairman 1977-1980)

My election to the Association Committee took place at the A.G.M. in 1972. The following year I became Treasurer (after Mr T. Forbes) and remained so until 1977 when I had the honour of being elected Chairman and continued in that office until 1980.

Congratulations

to

The
Cairngorm
Mountain Rescue
Association

on their

Silver Jubilee

*from the
Board of Directors,
Management, Staff and, of
course, the customers of
The Cairngorm Chairlift
Company*

The work of the Committee is, of course, mainly concerned with the welfare and well-being of the rescue team and the day-to-day problems of providing equipment, the control procedures and vehicle maintenance etc., but, in addition, other topics are discussed which are relevant to mountain rescue in a more general way.

Of the many topics debated I recall several in the period 1977-1980 which occupied a considerable amount of Committee time although not necessarily directly related to the operation of the team. For example, in 1979 we were visted by Rear-Admiral Dunbar-Naismith representing the Highlands and Islands Development Board in connection with the proposed ski development at Lurchers Gully. This resulted from concern expressed by the Committee that there might be an increase in rescue incidents. No doubt the concern still continues although as yet there have been no developments. In the same year considerable debate arose on the qualities and suitability of persons for recruitment following a request from the police that the size of the team should be increased. The formation of a ski group within the team at a cost of £800 also produced discussion, as did the request from the Police for the return of the garage used by the team for the Land Rover. The latter subject was eventually resolved by the construction of garages at the team's present headquarters at Achantoul. The demolition of Jean's Hut gave rise to varying opinions, much in the same way as the demolition of the bothies on the plateau had earlier. Other subjects, such as the constitution of the Mountain Rescue Committee of Scotland, also exercised the minds of the Committee members.

During the whole of my term on the Committee, and particularly during my period as Chairman, I enjoyed the help and co-operation of the Association and team members and I would especially thank Mollie Porter who was both Association Secretary and Team Leader throughout. Mountain rescue engenders a special relationship with other team members, many of whom I would not have otherwise met, and I appreciate enormously the friendship and fellowship and many happy hours which my involvement with the team produced. I extend to the present members my very best wishes for the future.

Chapter Five

1981 TO 1988

By Peter Cliff (Team Member since 1978 and Leader since 1981)

Mollie Porter's contribution to the Team was exceptional. For years she had been both Team Leader and Team Secretary, in effect running the Team single-handed. She also ran the Training Programme. Only she and her husband, Jo, know how much time she spent on the Team; but I expect it was more than any of us would care to guess. In the first four years of my spell as Team Leader (1981-4) I was fortunate to have Allan Bantick as Deputy Leader. Allan was Chief Instructor at R.A.F. Grantown Outdoor Centre, and so he brought to the Team a great knack for organisation and for generally getting things done. He took over the Training Programme and ran it extremely efficiently; and I don't think I could have taken on the workload of Leader without Allan's support in those early years. When he pulled out of the Team, John Allen and Graham Clarke were appointed as Joint Deputies; and I thank both of them for their support during these latter years.

During the period 1981-8 there have been three Chairmen (John Allen, Chris Barley and Dave Craig). All three have given me great support; I have always valued their advice; and I hope I continue to enjoy their close friendship for many more years to come.

The Eighties have seen a marked decrease in the number of people getting into problems due to poor clothing or equipment. On the other hand we have seen an increase in the number of people using skis away from the ski area. Skis are a very effective way of getting around snow covered mountains, and the Team's Ski Group (currently nine members using Alpine ski mountaineering equipment) is proof of that. The first time the Ski Group was used on a rescue we skied down the March Burn in poor weather conditions — it was a steep and difficult descent, involving an abseil with skis at one stage; and I doubt if any of us will forget it. The group was Dave Craig, Graham Clarke, Stuart Armstrong and me.

Unforgettable for other reasons was the occasion when John Gould climbed onto a table in the Red Macgregor Hotel. It was an unlikely event for two reasons: firstly, I do not recall anyone in the Team ever doing it before; and, secondly, up until that moment we had all thought of John as a quiet and gentle giant, the last person to perform such an extrovert act.

The occasion was a big search and we were switching areas after 12

Richard McHardy climbing the Cascade, Cairngorm. Photo by Peter Cliff.

James Grossett climbing The Icicle, Creag Dubh. Photo by Peter Cliff.

hours on the hill, so the Police fixed up a meal for us before we went out again. Jimmy Simpson is a Police dog handler and member of S.A.R-.D.A. and had been out with us. It was a long table, seating about 30 of us, with Jimmy at one end and John at the other. Jimmy was winding us up, telling us how good the Lochaber Team is, how they do this and how they do that. It was then that John did his party piece. He tiptoed down the table between the plates and glasses in his size 12 boots, stood over Jimmy, harangued him and then tiptoed back along the table to his chair. No damage caused, and the honour of the Team magnificently saved.

Another development in the Eighties has been the dramatic increase in climbing standards. The Team has matched that. In the winter of 1987/8 we have 12 people leading Winter Grade 5, and another six leading Grade 4. Most of our rescue work is floundering around in the dark or a blizzard or both, looking for someone, and climbing doesn't come into it; but when we do get a technical rescue it is sorted out by competent climbers who climb regularly together outside the Team. One of the results of this increased competence has been a slight change in role for the **R.A.F. Teams (Kinloss and Leuchars)**. They used to be called to practically every rescue in the Cairngorms, but now we can get local people in quicker. We still ask for their help with big searches and stretcher-carries, and so we still see them on most incidents and very much appreciate their presence. When a person is reported missing in the evening, the Cairngorm Team will frequently start the search during the night, with Kinloss and Leuchars coming in later that night or at dawn. We are very fortunate to have the support of these two skilled teams available to us.

The other big support we get from the R.A.F. is, of course, through the **R.A.F. Search and Rescue helicopters**. These are based at Lossiemouth (Sea Kings) and Leuchars (Wessex). Invariably we work with the Sea Kings, as Lossiemouth is so close to us; but we will get a Wessex in on the big rescues where two helicopters are required. The helicopter is a wonderful machine for mountain rescue. It can be used as a big taxi, getting teams into and out of areas; it can often fly straight into an area and pick the casualty up; it can search large areas of ground; and it can be used as an airborne radio relay. The R.A.F. always answer our requests for help, subject to their own operational jobs, mechanical problems and bad weather; and it can safely be said that, without this help, civilian teams like Cairngorm would no longer be able to cope with the workload.

The larger numbers in the Team and the increase in its competence has also led to a small change in the role of **Glenmore Lodge**. The staff of the Lodge used to play a major part on the hill and in controlling rescues. An obvious problem for the Lodge is that their courses must continue, and that does not happen too well if all the instructors are out on a rescue.

Due to its physical position, the Lodge can get people on to the hill very quickly; and so its main contribution at the moment is to get two or three very competent people out quickly, with the Cairngorm Team coming in later. Fred Harper left the Lodge in 1986, and with him went 17 years' experience of rescue in the Cairngorms. One of Fred's many attributes was a strangely reassuring voice on the radio. This was probably due to the fact that he kept calm, and you knew he had been through all this before.

The Police have statutory responsibility for mountain rescue, and so a Team Leader works closely with them, not only on rescues but also on other occasions. The Chief Inspectors since 1981 have been John Mac-Lean, Gordon Noble and currently Hugh Mackay, and the Team has enjoyed a most harmonious relationship with each in turn. On the subject of Chief Inspectors and flares, we accidentally put a parachute flare right across the front of John MacLean's car one night. A parachute flare goes 1,000ft. in the air before opening and lowering an illuminating flare on the end of a parachute. They are potentially lethal things in the wrong hands, and I wonder sometimes if ours are the right ones! We nearly shot down a Sea King helicopter with one, and on another occasion we may have contributed to the early demise of a cow!

But I digress. What we sometimes forget is that a rescue is a Police responsibility, which means that if anything goes wrong, they carry the proverbial can. And yet they have to sit back and watch us lot get stuck into the action. That they do this demonstrates the mutual trust which exists between the Police and the Team. There are two policemen who are members of the Team, and they play an important role in forging this trust. They are: Kenny Lindsay, currently Vice-Chairman and in charge of vehicles, and with whom I have worked closely on the organisation of many rescues; and Malcolm Sclater is one of the best climbers in the Team.

Many of the Team climb regularly together, sometimes going further afield to the Alps. John Allen's Volvo Estate was transporting four of us down the French Autoroute in the summer of 1986 when a Renault Alpini from the Rapid Intervention Brigade flagged us down. John and Chris Barley were snoozing in the back, I was in the passenger seat and one of the three above-named Police Officers was driving.

'Did the driver know that the limit on the French autoroutes was 130 k.p.h.?'

'Yes'.

'And did he know that he was doing 165 k.p.h.?'

'Yes'.

He was taken into the Police Station, and I was asked to go as well, in order to translate. We were taken to the Sergeant's Office, accompanied by the driver of the patrol car and two other Gendarmes. The questions were repeated, obtaining the same answers. The sergeant then said he was going to fine 'Monsieur le chauffeur' 600 French francs (about £60). This was coolly agreed upon, Monsieur le chauffeur obviously feeling flush with holiday money. A sheet of paper was fed into the sergeant's ancient typewriter.

'Registration mark of the vehicle, s'il vous plait'.

'Name of Monsieur le chauffeur, s'il vous plait'.

'Occupation of Monsieur le chauffeur, s'il vous plait'.

It suddenly dawned on me that being flush with holiday money might not be the only explanation for Monsieur le chauffeur's cool. Trying hard not to smile, I said:

'Monsieur le chauffeur est un gendarme en Ecosse'.

The sergeant stared at me like only Police sergeants can, but I didn't go red, nor did I smile. Eventually:

'Documentation, s'il vous plait'.

While my friend passed over his warrant card, one of the policemen quietly closed the door out onto the corridor. After a careful look at the warrant card, the sergeant handed it back, ripped the piece of paper out of the typewriter, threw it into the wastepaper basket and extended his hand in greeting, with:

'Ah, Camarade!'.

The Gauloises were passed round. No, they didn't climb; but one of them had gone skiing at Chamonix and recommended a little restaurant, where the food was superb. Yes, we would definitely go there, as we thought French food (and gendarmes) were the best in the world. We were duly escorted out to the car, where John and Chris were talking to two well dressed ladies, both of whom had that special look about them which you get when you've been kept waiting too long, but there's nothing you can do about it, and you are probably in the wrong anyway.

'Had we seen their husbands? They had been in there hours longer than us. Why were we out before them?'

'No, we hadn't seen their husbands; and the reason we were out before them was probably because we had agreed to the fine and their husbands were maybe arguing'.

With blue light flashing, the Renault Alpini escorted us the wrong way up the slip road (to save us time) and back onto the autoroute; and we sent them a postcard from Chamonix.

Achantoul Base. As Dave Morris (Area Officer for the Nature Conservancy Council) left my office, a thought occurred: "Have you any room in that mansion of yours for a mountain rescue team?" He looked at me as if

I'd been sent from Heaven, the answer to his prayers, the solution to an impossible problem. It is the only time an N.C.C. officer has equated me to a Heavenly Body. But a few months later we moved into Achantoul, a move which was to everyone's advantage. The Police were already cramped in the Aviemore Station and faced the prospect of worse things to come, as the Sub Divisional Headquarters were to move from Kingussie to Aviemore. Obviously they needed as much space as possible, which included our store and garage. In fact, we had already outgrown the limited space we had in the Police Station; and so a move would suit both parties. The N.C.C. occupied Achantoul, a fine house on the outskirts of Aviemore, once owned by Seton Gordon. There was pressure coming from within the N.C.C. to make better use of the building; and this 'better use' came in the shape of the Meteorological Office, who set up a 24 hour weather recording station there, and ourselves.

We built a large 4-bay garage for the vehicles, and in the main house we have a storeroom, use of a lecture/meeting room, and use of a small lounge. Before going out on a rescue we can pop in to the Met. Office and check the current wind strength, wind direction and temperature on the summit of Cairngorm, as they have readouts from two weather stations up there. Helicopters land on the field opposite; and so, all in all, it is a most convenient base for us. The only disadvantage is that we are physically away from the Police Station, which means slightly less contact with the Police on a regular basis. As I write this, a new Police Station is being built, so, who knows, maybe we'll move back one day.

Call-Out System. What happens in the very early stages depends on the location of the incident. If it is in the Northern Corries it is governed by a Police procedural document (Appendix A of Police Order P.137) by which the Police telephone the Principal of Glenmore Lodge and the Leader of the Cairngorm Team, or their Deputies, and a Control Unit of these two plus a Police Officer is then set up. The only exception to this is a minor incident, where a Team call-out will not be required. For all other areas the Police telephone the Leader of the Cairngorm Team. So what actually happens is that an initial plan is made over the telephone. It may be decided to call the whole team straight away; or to send out a small number of the team, say in the night, with the rest called for a pre-dawn start; or to call a limited number of good climbers, say for a technical rescue where we are pretty certain that a helicopter will be able to help. We might decide to wait a while, to give the missing people the chance to walk out, or to give the Police longer to check car parks, bars, etc.

If someone has reported a friend(s) overdue, the Police will have already talked to them; but we usually like to do that too, which probably means that I go up to the Police Station. A lot of information can often be assembled this way, so helping with subsequent difficult decisions about where to search.

In these early stages helicopter assistance will also be considered and any requests for help are made to the Rescue Co-ordinating Centre at Pitreavie Castle just outside Edinburgh. Likewise, if we think search dogs might be useful we will decide how many we might need and will then request them through the Search and Rescue Dog Association. Two team members currently have dogs and are members of S.A.R.D.A., and a third is being trained. If extra manpower is going to be needed, we will phone the R.C.C. at Pitreavie Castle to see if we can get the help of R.A.F. Kinloss or R.A.F. Leuchars Mountain Rescue Teams.

By this time I will have spoken to John Allen, Deputy Leader, and will have agreed a plan with him. If we decide to call the team out, I then make five phone calls. Appendix 4 is the 1988 Call-Out List and shows this procedure. The first is to Chris Barley, asking him to go to Achantoul and to prepare whatever equipment we think we might need. The others are to the four callers-out. The message might be to meet straight away at Achantoul; or, say, for a pre-dawn start around 0500 hours. It is always possible that, in the meantime, a missing party turns up; and if we are unable to reach all the Team members to cancel the Call-Out it can result in someone arriving at Achantoul in the early hours of a winter morning to find the place deserted, except for a brief note on the storeroom door saying "Call-Out cancelled".

The minimum standard for entry into the team is, as a guideline, 'committed winter hillwalker'. Most of the work involves floundering around in bad weather or the dark, or both, so we need people who can cope with that, who can navigate, and who can move competently on steep ground. In addition we need some climbers for technical rescues, and we currently have 12 who climb at winter grade 5. We are well covered on the medical side, with three doctors in the team at the moment. The Grantown-on-Spey practice supports us particularly well, guaranteeing either Dr Peter Grant or Dr Leslie Cowan on any Call-Out. The Spey Valley is a tourist area, so there is quite a movement of people in and out of the Valley, even among those who are here for longer than a season. This means that the numbers fluctuate around the 45 mark, with 50 being the self-imposed maximum at the moment. It is no bad thing that we get an annual change of membership — a little new blood never does any harm. Sometimes people are surprised to see women in the team, but I do not see why. When people apply to join the team they are judged purely on their mountaineering competence — and personality comes into it a bit as well. We have nine women members at the moment, and they do the same job as their male colleagues.

Training. The team's own Training Programme operates on one Thursday evening and one Sunday, each month. The programme has four objectives: (1) to train team members in rescue skills; (2) to give them an opportunity to increase their own personal mountaineering skills; (3) to pass on new skills, information or developments of any kind; and (4) to get out mountaineering together away from the pressure of a rescue, so that we all know each other as well as possible. In addition to our own programme, we help members financially to go on relevant courses, e.g. mountain rescue, avalanche courses, snow and ice climbing, rock climbing, mountain leader training and assessment, Mountaineering Instructor's Certificate, First Aid, etc., etc.

RESCUES 1981-1988

The following incidents illustrate different aspects of the Team's work during the period 1981-88:

Hell's Lum, 31st December 1981

My telephone woke me at 0730 in the morning: the Team was involved in a rescue on Hell's Lum; the Police had been phoning me since midnight, but I had been sleeping deeply, oblivious to events high in the Cairngorms that cold and stormy January morning. I arrived at Glenmore Lodge in time to listen in on the radio to the final stages of a dramatic incident.

Five students from a London College started climbing Escalator on the previous day, Wednesday. Four of them climbed roped as two pairs, while the fifth, an experienced climber, went solo without a rope. He reached the top and waited for the others. But they were having trouble, and when it got dark he lowered a rope to them.

By 9 pm there was still no sign of them, so he went for help. A blizzard was now blowing and he had a desperate walk out, but eventually raised the alarm around midnight. Six of the Cairngorm Team with 2 S.A.R-.D.A. dogs left Glenmore Lodge soon after 2 am, followed about 6.30 am by another 8, Ado Liddell from the Lodge and an R.A.F. Leuchars party.

Meanwhile, three of the others had reached the top, but were unable to pull the fourth up. They were just getting into their bivouac bags when a particularly vicious gust of wind hit them, and one of them was blown back over the crag. Tony Flood and dog, Graham Clarke and Iain Smith found him at 5.50 am at the foot of the crag, in a slightly shredded poly bag and hypothermic, but, as it turned out, otherwise none the worse for wear after his 900 foot fall. He mumbled something about having fallen 30

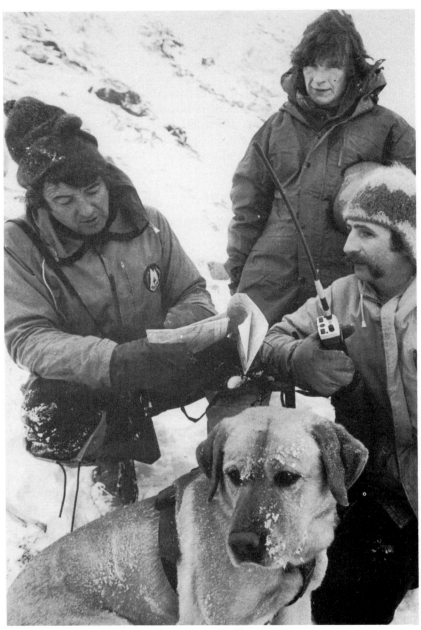

L to R: John Allen, Moira Snadden, Graham Clarke and Sam. Photo by The Sunday Express.

Cableway Rescue in Coire an t-Sneachda. Photo by John Lyall.

Group with Terri track vehicle. Photo by Ann Wakeling.

Land Rover crossing River Einich. Photo by John Armstrong.

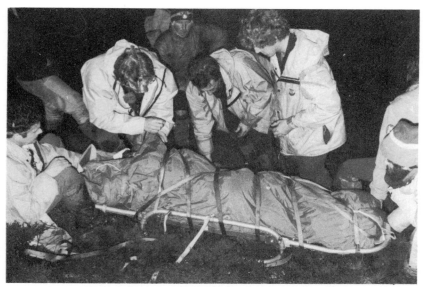

Casualty being prepared for helicopter winch on rescue of 9th October 1982. L to R: Jimmy Simpson, Peter Cliff, Ado Liddell, Mick Taylor (RAF), Ian Peter, Graham Clarke, and Iain Smith (with hat). Photo by Harry Travers.

Graham Clarke taking the ski stretcher down steep ground. Photo by Ian Southern.

feet or so. When Graham and Iain climbed back up the slope to the foot of the crag they found a boot and gaiter, which in fact did not belong to this man — and a big hole in the snow where he had landed.

The other Cairngorm party with Ado Liddell found two at the top of the crag; and shortly after that they retrieved the body of the fifth student from lower down on the climb. He had died of hypothermia, and had demonstrated the curious behaviour of 'paradoxical undressing' or 'mountain disrobing syndrome', whereby as the victim begins to lose consciousness, he may develop a feeling of warmth, to such an extent that he undresses or climbs out of a sleeping bag. The boot and gaiter found at the foot of the crag in fact belonged to the one who died.

The two at the top were able to walk out with the team; and the one at the bottom was airlifted out, thanks to superb flying by Flt.Lt. David Simpson who managed to land his Sea King near the Shelter Stone in conditions not normally associated with flying helicopters.

Lurcher's Crag, 10th October 1982

The Cairngorm Team deals with relatively few cases of seriously injured climbers who are still alive, as a complicating factor in many, if not most, of our incidents is bad weather. A climber who falls and sustains serious injuries in bad weather will inevitably become hypothermic, maybe fatally so. A recent case, November 1987, illustrates the point: a mountaineer fell down Stac an Fharaidh overlooking Loch Avon and broke his back; but he died not from that, but from hypothermia. A happier result occurred on 10th October 1982, when a walker fell about 70 feet down the Lurcher's Crag into the Lairig Ghru as he tried to find his way down off Ben Macdui in thick mist. His companion ran out to raise the alarm; and shortly afterwards a Sea King picked up a party from the Team. It only managed to take us a short way because of thick mist, and so we continued on foot, while the helicopter returned to Glenmore Lodge and shut down, waiting to see if it could help us later on. The friend had been unable to pinpoint the exact place, so we had to search the whole of that flank of the Lairig Ghru. The night was dark; and the ground steep, wet and slippery. It was difficult to keep a straight line of searchers. While we did this, Martin Burrows-Smith and Iain Peter from Glenmore Lodge searched the rim of the plateau above.

Just before 3 am Graham Clarke, who was on one end of the line, found him — lying face down and deeply unconscious. We had no doctor with us; but we had recently run the Dr Ieuan Jones Mountain First Aid Course for the Team, a course which is much more advanced than standard courses and which was to prepare us for just such an occasion.

Graham and I examined our unconscious casualty, and then we compared notes: we both agreed that he had a fractured skull and fractured spine, and of course was hypothermic. By this time we had been joined by the Glenmore Lodge staff and the R.A.F. Kinloss Team, so we had plenty of manpower. But a stretcher carry from high up on this steep ground would have been extremely hazardous to someone with these injuries. The helicopter was the answer, if only it could get in. As it happened the mist was clearing slightly. It seemed to be going through in banks, with clearer spells in between. It was still pitch dark.

The Sea King crew agreed over the radio to give it a try; and it wasn't long before we heard its engines; and then we saw its powerful lights probing the mist. The Kinloss Team released some flares to indicate our position; and then the helicopter was right above us, like some enormous ship from Star Wars, with its banks of lights illuminating the hillside around us. The winchman was lowered to us, and within seconds he was on his way back up again, guiding the stretcher into the helicopter. The next stop for them was Aberdeen Royal Infirmary, where the diagnosis was confirmed: fractured spine, double fractured skull and hypothermia. I believe he went on to make a good recovery.

John Allen, Brian Gallagher and Police dog during search of 26th March 1984.
Photo by Ann Wakeling.

49

Team Members at Jean's Hut 1982. L to R: Dave Broadhead, Frank Allen, Harry Travers, Andy Smith (kneeling), Harry Jamieson, Digby Bulmer, Alex Sutherland, Steve Travers, Allan Bantick, Peter Cliff, Paul Rennie, Sue Jardine, Chris Barley, Ann Wakeling, Willie Anderson, Peter Grant. Photo by Harry Travers.

Daydream, Coire an Lochain, 21st February 1983

When a climber falls from 100 feet above his friend and if he has no intermediate running belays, he will fall 200 feet; which is exactly what happened to two climbers on Daydream — an ice climb in Coire an Lochain. The leader broke his leg (mid-shaft of femur). It was late in the afternoon and as darkness fell they reflected that, although things could be better, they could also be a lot worse — at least they had a really good belay.

At 8.15 pm three staff from Glenmore Lodge (Sam Crymble, Mark Diggins and Colin Firth) were flown in by Sea King, followed shortly by four members of the Cairngorm Team (Malcolm Sclater, Roger Gaff, Dave Broadhead and me). Having landed us on the frozen lochan, the helicopter returned to Glenmore Lodge to refuel.

The stretcher we had was a Piguillem, normally an ideal stretcher but too short for this particular casualty, who was a big man. We had a Hare traction splint for the broken leg, but fitting it looked first of all difficult and then impossible — standing there on the front points of one's crampons in the dark. The helicopter had returned to the lochan and had radioed that they could only wait a short time as their rotors were freezing up. The splint was impossible, so we shoved the Entonox bottle (pain relieving gas) down inside the casualty bag and showed the casualty how to use it. As we started to lower, his heels, which were sticking out beyond the stretcher, dug into the snow, so we turned the stretcher onto its side with the broken leg uppermost. This worked well and we were able to lower 750 ft. on single ropes from a deadman belay (alloy plate hammered into the snow to act as an anchor), including going over a short craggy section where the stretcher was hanging free with Malcolm and me attached to it. Not many people would have the courage to laugh and joke in such a situation, but that is exactly what this injured climber did throughout the entire rescue.

John Allen and Dave Craig, with 10 other members of the Team, had meanwhile come in on foot and skis, meeting us on the lower slopes and helping us get the stretcher into the helicopter. As it flew the injured man away to Raigmore at Inverness, I wondered what we would do without helicopters, Entonox and deadmen.

January 1984

This must count as one of the busiest periods of the Team's history to date, with eight incidents and 1000 manhours in less than four weeks. It started on **New Year's Day** with a search for two climbers from Swansea University Climbing Club. Allan Bantick, John Gould, Iain Ross, Chris and Denise Barley and dog searched overnight; and another big party from the team met the two at 8.45 am next morning, making their way safely off the hill, having bivouaced at the top of the Fiacaill of Coire Cas.

On **5th January** a 24-year-old Spanish climber went climbing on his own in Coire an t-Sneachda, but got lost on his way out as he had neither map nor compass. A search involving the Team, Glenmore Lodge, 3 S.A.R.D.A. dogs, R.A.F. Kinloss and a Sea King continued through the night to the next morning, when he was found at Bynack Stable, cold and tired but unhurt.

That same day, **Friday 6th**, a 33-year-old walker from Bristol went for a walk up the Lairig Ghru. He set off at midday with four hours of daylight left, wearing light boots, a duvet and overtrousers, but with no ice axe, no crampons, no map, no compass, no torch, and no bivouac equipment. He had been offered a map in Aviemore, but had refused it; and he had declined advice on what might be a suitable walk. He had what he thought was a weather forecast and which was 'GOOD' — but this was the state of the ski runs, on the indicator board in Coire Cas car park. When he was reported overdue that evening we started a search with little idea of where to begin. At 9 am the next morning he turned up at Tomintoul, having walked up the Lairig Ghru, climbed the March Burn (plastered in snow), down to Loch Avon (believing he was descending into Coire an Lochain), and on to Tomintoul — a distance of 42 kilometres.

51

For most of the time he had had no idea where he was or where he was going, and he was not in the least concerned that people had been worried for him.

A few days later, **15th January**, we had a much more serious incident. A 46-year-old teacher from a school in Surrey, took six boys aged 15-17 climbing in Coire an Lochain. They were well clothed and had bivouac equipment in their rucsacks; but the teacher decided to leave the boys' rucsacks in Jean's Hut, which at that time stood in the coire. They set off to climb the Couloir, a Grade 1 snow climb. As they set foot on the climb, another climber came scooting past them, having been avalanched out of a neighbouring route. Having picked himself up, he advised the teacher and the boys against climbing any higher, as there was an obvious avalanche risk. This advice was ignored.

They successfully completed the climb, and started to return to the hut, the teacher navigating in front. He should have gone on a bearing of approximately West and then North, but it seems he had his compass the wrong way round, because he ended up going East. Darkness fell; and they eventually stumbled into Bynack Stable hut at 1 am, having no idea where they were until they read the name of the hut. A search was just being started at this time, with the first of the Glenmore staff leaving the Lodge at 2 am. It was a pity the teacher did not come on down to the Lodge, as he could have reached it in an hour, and so prevented the whole incident escalating. What he did was to stay in the hut and to then saunter in at 8 am to Glenmore Lodge, where Allan Bantick found him quietly helping himself to the public phone.

When somebody has made a bad mistake, we will probably have a quiet word with them in private, pointing out in a constructive way what we think went wrong. In this case it was put to the teacher that he had made three mistakes: he had left the boys' rucsacks with their emergency bivouac equipment in Jean's Hut; he had got his navigation badly wrong, and he should have walked out at 1 am to Glenmore Lodge. What of course made the matter all the more serious was that this was a case of an adult with clear responsibility for a group of school children. At this point we did not know about the other climber being avalanched, and that of course showed that the teacher continued in the face of very obvious and real avalanche danger. We suggested he had been lucky to get away with it, and that before he took the boys out again, he should brush up on his navigation and reconsider some of his decision making. The teacher refused to accept these points at all, saying: "I would do the same again".

Most rescues attract media interest, and this was no exception. One policy with the media is to slam the door as hard and fast as possible, hoping to catch the odd finger or camera lens in the process. All that this results in, is the journalist ferreting around elsewhere and producing a factually inaccurate article or making it up altogether. Our policy is to co-operate as much as possible, to give them as much of the facts and background as we can (within certain restraints), so that hopefully the public gets a well-balanced and accurate account of the incident. Frequently I am invited to level criticism, an invitation which is dissidously avoided as our job is rescue not retribution. But I believe there are cases which are so serious that it would be wrong to keep quiet, where the rescue services must say: "Look, this was really bad, and I tell you why." This was one such case, because when an adult takes other people's children into the mountains in winter, he takes on an added responsibility; and if he does not recognise that, then the situation is very serious. indeed.

The media had a story, and they used it. It was the main front-page item on many national dailies. Later on there were letters in the mountaineering publications expressing concern, not that children might be at risk in the mountains, but that Fred and I had dared to suggest it. The British Mountaineering Council pompously suggested that they should set up a Media Supremo: on rescues all media questions would be answered by him, in Manchester. I had just one question for the B.M.C.: who was going to brief him?

One final point: the group was carrying a CB radio. We knew this and tried repeatedly to contact them on it. They also had tried to contact us. No contact was ever made; so this incident does not strengthen the argument that CB radios would increase safety on the hills.

Saturday, 21st January started with a straightforward evacuation of an injured farmer from his farm. During the night the wind had steadily gone into the South and had increased, drifting the large accumulations of dry snow which lay on the mountains and in the fields. By midday the wind at Aviemore was averaging 23 knots with gusts of 40 knots, Cairngorm top chairlift average was 50 knots with gusts of 80 knots. I planned to be back home in time for lunch, but, with the exception of one brief stop, didn't make it until Monday night. The strong winds had started to drift snow onto the roads, and the Police asked us to help them to reach trapped motorists on Drumochter. We agreed to do this as a quick in-and-out job, as members of the Dundee Rucsack Club had said to us that they were concerned about three of their members who had gone up to the Sinclair Hut that morning. By this time (mid-afternoon) the conditions were so bad that a mountain search was ruled out as impossible, and we decided to review the situation again in the morning.

Taking the Land Rover and 4-wheel drive Transit, and together with a snowplough and Police Land Rover, we worked our way down the A9, checking cars and taking people into our vehicles. The wind was so strong that we were being blown over on the road whenever we got out of the vehicles.The driver of the snowplough handled the big machine with great skill, manoeuvering it carefully between half-buried vehicles. But it was only a matter of time before the inevitable happened, and we all got stuck. Kenny Lindsay, Ken Taylor and I settled down for the night in the Transit with a Policeman and 10 rescued motorists. It was going to be important to keep the engine going, and so I had turned the vehicle round with its back to the wind. At 8 pm the wind at the Cairngorm top chairlift station was averaging 71 knots with gusts of 93. We were joined about 1 am by Graham Clarke, Chris Barley and James Grossett who had come in on the Terri tracked vehicle — for them the visibility had been so poor that Chris and James had had to walk ahead with avalanche probes, probing to find the tarmac of the dual carriageway. Even so they had lost the road and at one point nearly drove over a 20 ft. culvert.

During this night wind speeds of 161 m.p.h. were recorded on Cairngorm summit. The three-and-a-half ton roof of the bottom chairlift station was lifted off and deposited 100 yards away, snapping in half steel fasteners which had held the roof in place for 18 years.

Sunday, 22nd January. By dawn the wind had eased off (Cairngorm top chairlift average 44 knots with gusts of 58 at 6 am, and Aviemore average 23 with gusts of 42). We found we were just opposite Dalwhinnie. Using the Terri and some shovels we dug 150 people out of their vehicles and walked them to the village; and the Police borrowed a stranded train to extract a futher 300 from Drumochter Lodge. A phone call from Fred Harper and worrying news: the Dundee group was still missing, and in addition there was concern for a group from Heriot-Watt. I promised to get round as soon as the roads were cleared, and Fred would meanwhile phone the rest of the Team and try to get them to the Lodge. Travel had by this time come to a complete halt, and the R.A.F. helicopters were inundated with emergency calls.

The Team was subsequently awarded the Royal Humane Society's Honorary Testimonial inscribed on vellum:

> ". . . for having on the 21st and 22nd January 1984 gone to the rescue of people trapped in severe storm conditions in North Scotland, and whose lives they gallantly saved".

When we arrived at Glenmore Lodge later that day, Sunday 22nd, the news was terrible: the Dundee group was still missing, and the group from Heriot-Watt had got into trouble — three dead and one survivor. They had set out on Friday night to reach Jean's Hut. When they failed to reach the hut in deteriorating conditions, they pitched their Vango tent at 2.30 am, intending to return to the car park on Saturday morning. They tried to do this, but had to bivouac a second night on the way back, by the Sneachda burn. Three of them died, including two brothers. The sole survivor managed to stagger out onto the ski road and down to Glenmore Lodge. Glenmore Lodge staff, an R.A.F. helicopter, a PLM helicopter and R.A.F. Leuchars recovered the bodies.

At 5.15 pm the Army reported concern about two of their men who had gone out on Friday on a two-night snowholing exercise. Both men were strong and well equipped, and one of them was very experienced, being an instructor with the Joint Services Mountain Training Centre. We decided to start a search at first light, and because many of the roads were still impassable due to fallen trees and drifted snow, we spent the night on the floor of our base at Achantoul.

At 6.45 pm the Dundee party were reported in safe and well.

Monday 23rd January. The Team went out on the hill at dawn, together with R.A.F. Kinloss, R.A.F. Leuchars, staff from Glenmore Lodge and 6 S.A.R.D.A. dogs. The wind increased rapidly. Statistics from the Chairlift top station show it peaked around 1 pm, averaging 33 knots with gusts of 47; but locally it was much stronger than that, to the extent that several teams came off the hill before midday, and at 11 am the R.A.F. said the conditions were outside helicopter operational limits. Jimmy Simpson's dog Rocky was blown over the edge of Coire an t-Sneachda, to be found the next day by Jimmy none the worse for wear. Visibility was poor in driving snow, the avalanche risk was exceptionally high, and we were continually knocked over by the wind, occasionally being picked up and thrown down again a few yards away.

Tuesday 24th January. The search resumed at first light with a large party of the Team being flown in to probe the snowhole site at Feith Buidhe, where the soldiers had planned to snowhole on the Friday night. We felt it was a forlorn task, as something like 60 ft of snow had drifted in and our 14 ft probes were a token gesture. S.A.R.D.A. dogs, J.S.M.T.C. staff and R.A.F. Leuchars searched other areas. That night I withdrew the Team from the search, as I felt that there was no chance the soldiers had survived and we desperately needed to rest in case of another incident.

The search was continued the next day by the military, and on Thursday the bodies were found by friends of one of the soldiers who went straight to the site. A psychic medium in Derbyshire had given them the following message:

'On a ridge, pretty high up — perhaps near the cornice at the top. He's looking through 3-4 trees to a big lake and seeing a wideish stretch of water. He's in a bivvy sack covered in snow with a very small opening, looking sharply down to a ridge that is diagonal to him. The ridge juts out and rock can be seen.

He has heard a helicopter, which has flown overhead but perhaps because of the cornice hasn't seen the hole. The rescue team have prodded the area but not far enough up. He's a very experienced mountaineer and managed to dig himself into the slope very high.'

They interpreted the water as being Loch Morlich, the ridge as being the Fiacaill of Sneachda, and that they were therefore high on the headwall of Sneachda or Lochain, close to the Fiacaill. They found them high on the headwall of Sneachda, between the Goat Track and the Fiacaill, under the cornice, one of them in a bivvy sack. A helicopter had flown over them several times, and one team had been searching the slope directly below them until they had been avalanched off. There are three isolated trees in the stream draining down from Castle hill.

Group on Cairngorm Plateau. L to R: Andy Smith, Kenny Lindsay, Harry Travers, and Ann Wakeling.

Probing Avalanche Debris. Photo by The Sunday Express.

Avalanche Crownwall, Coire Cas, 1988. Photo by Peter Cliff.

MAIL PLANE. For some of us the longest continual period on a single search was when a Bandirante Mail plane went missing, shortly after take-off from Inverness Airport on Monday, 19th November 1984. Starting on the Tuesday morning at 6 am we continued until 2 am on the Wednesday — 20 hours continuous searching. The pilot was killed and his employers, friends and relatives gave money to the Team, with which we established a Memorial Training Fund, using the income each year for specific training purposes. It often happens that during and after an incident I speak to relatives on the telephone and exchange letters. The pilot's mother was in touch with me often to find out more about the incident and to discuss ways in which the money should be spent. We met each other in London, and later in the summer she came to stay with us and I took her out to Saddle Hill, the scene of the crash. We still exchange letters, maybe twice a year.

BEN MACDUI. If you are going to bivouac on the Cairngorm Plateau in a winter storm and walk out the next morning, I cannot think of a more appropriate name than Tough or Hardy; and yet these were truly the names of two Royal Navy men who did just that in February 1987! The Team's involvement included 5 members of the ski group searching in the night, with Graham Clarke's dog Sam. Roger Gaff, Eric Pirie and I ended up sheltering in a snowhole in Coire Domhain in the early hours of the morning, thanks to the hospitality of the incumbents. Tough and Hardy lived up to their names and walked down in the morning, having themselves bivouacked in a snowhole; and what a field day the Press had with names like that!

They had been on their way back from Ben Macdui, a mountain which to my certain knowledge has been the scene of at least two family rows, resulting in people stomping off in different directions — but with only one compass between them! Mediating between the warring factions once all are safe and well is, I suppose, part of the mountain rescue role!

GEAL CHARN. In the early stages of some incidents we are literally confronted with searching the whole of the Cairngorms. It may be that a party has been reported overdue and there is no indication as to where they might be — except in the Cairngorms. This is where time spent in research or detective work is time well spent. Kenny Lindsay and I did this on the night of 7th/8th March 1987. Kenny is both a Team member and a Policeman, and we have worked closely together in the co-ordination of several rescues. At the start of this incident, about 10 pm on the Saturday night, we did not even know which mountain the missing people might be on; but by following up phone calls and gradually piecing information together, we worked out that they might have gone up Geal Charn as it had not been ticked off in the Munros Tables. Knowing the time they had left their guesthouse, we worked out a possible time for getting to the top; and that coincided with a cold front passing through the area. A possibility was that they had been hit by bad weather while trying to descend and had fallen over the cornice. Their car was found at the road end, as near to Geal Charn as possible. The Team went straight up into the coire where a large amount of fresh avalanche debris was found. The two bodies were found here, confirming the possibility that they had fallen through the cornice, so triggering an avalanche on the scarp slope below.

A month later, at the request of one of the relatives, a Team member scattered the ashes of the two casualties on the summit of Geal Charn.

GLEN FESHIE. When another team comes in to help us the Team Leader is invited to join the Control Unit, since his own experience will be invaluable in the decision making process and he knows his own team better than anyone. On 31st August and 1st July 1987 we had a big search for two Boy Scouts over 2 days involving over 80 people from Cairngorm, Kinloss, Leuchars, Braemar, Aberdeen, 4 S.A.R.D.A. dogs and 2 RAF helicopters. Our control was based in a caravan at the Glen Feshie Gliding Club, generously handed over to us for the duration by the members of the club. Flight Sergeant Dave Whalley, Team Leader of Leuchars (known to everyone as 'Heavy'), and Cpl. Derek Scott from Kinloss ('Scottie') joined Kenny and me as the Control Unit. The search had started at 1200 on the Friday when I flew in a Sea King from Lossiemouth over the boys' intended route. A total of 51 from Cairngorm, Kinloss and Leuchars went out at 3 pm, being joined by a further 26 from Braemar and Aberdeen at 6 am on the Saturday. As we progressively failed to find the boys, so the search area was widened. By widening the area we were going into the less likely areas, and we became more and more concerned for the safety of the boys.

At 7 pm, Saturday, the teams were coming down off the hill, and we were finalising plans to bring in even more searchers for the next day (7 teams, 120 searchers, 8 dogs, 4 helicopters). The Sea King was making a final sweep on the south side of the Feshie, the area we were going into the next day, when the crew spotted the boys. They were cold, hungry, tired and frightened but otherwise safe and well. They had got lost, strayed off their map, and had been there since Thursday.

That was one of the best rescues I have been involved in, because just at the moment when we were all dispirited and giving up hope, we found them.

The Future

Bristows Helicopters did some sums in 1987 and said they could run the helicopter Search and Rescue service for £26 million per annum, i.e. 45% of the £57 million quoted in Parliament as being the existing cost to the RAF. They propose that their helicopters would be under contract to the Department of Transport, just as their Stornoway and Sumburgh helicopters are under contract to HM Coastguard. Lots of questions have been thrown up, and fully or partly aired, like: insurance, professionalisation, costs. Few people doubt that Bristows have the helicopters and the crews, but a big concern is that the RAF be allowed to maintain a full and active part so that they are always prepared for both their peacetime and wartime roles. The Government has turned down Bristows on this occasion, but that does not rule out further consideration in the future. In any case, the teams on the West Coast are already working with the Bristows' helicopter at Stornoway.

As I write this, there is talk of the Wessex helicopter squadron at RAF Leuchars being moved elsewhere. So it seems that the Zeebrugge Ferry Disaster has affected even Mountain Rescue in the North of Scotland, as Government realises the dire lack of big rescue helicopters on the South Coast of England and juggles resources accordingly.

The Cairngorm Team's main area of operation (Cairngorm, Ben Macdui, Braeriach) is an area attracting a vast amount of conservation interest. The ski development on Cairngorm has been the nucleus of this interest, resulting in the usual polarising of views. People are labelled 'skier', 'mountaineer' or 'conservationist'. Has it never occurred to these antagonists that the same man or woman can actually indulge in all three? The Team has to operate in this sensitive area and we have already taken some flak for using a tracked vehicle and for running our Sponsored Walk through the Lairig Ghru. That it will become more sensitive and that we will take more flak is probably inevitable, but the job of a mountain rescue team is to rescue injured and lost people in the hills. And if a helicopter or tracked vehicle will make a life saving contribution it will be used — and if the mosses, lichens or snow buntings are disturbed, then so be it.

What about the Lairig Ghru Walk? For some years now the finances of the Team have been dependent on the Sponsored Walk. We recognise that, on that day, the peace and quiet might be spoilt for other walkers, but our event is well publicised in advance and we have had no complaints from other walkers. In any case, surely it is a matter of balance and proportion? Some people who do our Walk would not otherwise walk the Lairig Ghru, so they gain in experience; others wait and plan to do the

'Lairig' on our Walk; everyone has the satisfaction of working hard for a voluntary body (a charity), and of putting something back into the system. It costs a lot of money to keep nearly 50 men and women trained, clothed and equipped; and that money doesn't just come in through the letterbox — you have to go out and get it. One hardline conservationist wrote to me that we should replace the Walk with a sponsored ditch clearing day! I told him it was just as well he wasn't our Treasurer.

The number of incidents increases steadily — some years up, some years down, but definitely an overall increase — presumably due to increased leisure time and higher emphasis on sport and healthy living. A linear projection of the Scottish incidents as a whole show that by 1998 we will be dealing with double the 1982 incidents. Eventually this projection will flatten out, but in the meantime, can teams cope? If the extra workload is spread out over the year, we probably can; but if it comes bunched up with existing busy periods (New Year, sudden storms after a spell of clear weather, weekends, etc) then the Team may have to adjust. A Team of 50 members may be able to cope, subject to the commitment of individual members and the agreement of employers to release people — but there is a limit to what can reasonably be expected from both. This particularly applies to Team members who have an extra commitment to the Team; and if the workload of, say, a Team Leader increases in proportion to the incidents, then I believe some direct financial compensation may be necessary in the future.

Whatever developments and changes take place in the future, I don't think the nature of mountain rescue in this country will ever change. It will always be done by volunteer men and women, who simply want to help fellow mountaineers in trouble.

A CHAIRMAN'S VIEW

By David Craig (Team Member since 1977 and Chairman since 1986)

When elected to any committee office many of us must consider our election with mixed feelings. These feelings may well range between, "What an honour", to "Oh no! Not another committee — something else to keep me off the hill", to "Why me? Is it because they know I have access to an electric typewriter?" In this case trepidation also came into it, as I was not only to take on a position of great responsibility but, far more significant, had to follow in the footsteps of one of our elder statesmen, probably one of the greatest diplomats ever to be found in the ranks of mountain rescue (certainly within the Cairngorm Team) — Christopher Barley.

Committees tend to have a reputation of being rather dry, boring affairs, but not so the Cairngorm Mountain Rescue Association (C.M.R.A.), certainly not since May 1986. My first meeting, in June 1986, had a full, indeed varied, agenda including many interesting items. Around a dozen Team members had recently returned from the cliffs of Cornwall, having had a very fruitful week's climbing accompanied by members of staff from Glenmore Lodge. The Goretex material supplied free of charge through the generosity of W.L. Gore Ltd. was well on its way to being stitched up by Snowdon Mouldings and would soon be ready for testing by the Team. This was one instance where one might say the Team were working from hand to mouth. A certain gentleman, at that time working for W.L. Gore, had had the misfortune to suffer toothache whilst resident in Strathspey. As many readers may know, Chris Barley is a dentist, and happened to be the person called to treat him. Becoming quickly aware of his influential position with the fabric company Chris worked effectively on more than his patient's carious canines. Treatment and a deal were satisfactorily completed simultaneously.

Not without a little sadness it was recorded at this early meeting that Jean's Hut, the little refuge in Coire an Lochain, which had suffered much misuse and abuse in recent years, had finally been removed earlier in June that year. Still on the theme of buildings, the meeting in June 1986 saw discussed, because of rising Team numbers and overcrowding on indoor training evenings, the possibility of extending/rearranging our accommodation at Achantoul. This potentially straight road leading to future development and convenience soon proved to be something of a twisting route leading to an ultimate cul-de-sac, since it transpired that the C.M.R.A. had not actually received or signed a lease agreement mutually acceptable to the C.M.R.A. and the sitting tenants, the Nature Conservancy Council, despite the fact that the Team had been making use of the building since 1983. Because of the need to finalise a lease agreement it was decided to initiate the formalisation of the situation. There then followed much lengthy correspondence between the C.M.R.A. and N.C.C., and after many hours of committee time being spent on the matter a sub-committee, later known as the Triumphant Triumvirate, was elected (who said this Chairmanship was easy?!) and the matter was finally resolved in June 1987.

Willie Anderson, just returned from a year in Tasmania, bravely took on the responsibility of convening the sub-committee to organise the 1987 sponsored walk through the Lairig Ghru. The walk was once again a great success, raising in excess of £30,000. Again thanks to all those who worked for and supported our efforts on that event.

Avalanche transceivers constitute another of these "on going" matters arising. After many years of using Pieps, first I, then II, and now Dual Frequency, the Association has opted to convert to the Autophon system, the first consignment having arrived in December 1987.

Yet another somewhat sad farewell was said in January 1988 when the Team parted with the "old" long wheel base, white Land Rover, gifted over fourteen years ago through a sponsorship kindly arranged by the Grant's Whisky Company. The vehicle had served the Team well over the years but was becoming, as with any older vehicle, increasingly in need of repair. Also it was somewhat sluggish on road journeys, a major consideration when the Team does have an increased involvement in snow-blocked road rescue and the old Rover was without a heater. For the moment the replacement comes in the form of a four-wheel drive Bedford van which has already proved very versatile in terms of towing and personnel carrying capacity.

The Team raises funds in many ways. In 1984 we helped Ford Motor Co. to make a TV advertisement for Transits.

Radio communication has long been a problem for Mountain Rescue Teams, and is another item which has involved our Association in many hours of debate. The main issues being that of whether to press for F.M. or A.M. and then whether high-band or low-band frequency. Not one meeting has gone by during the past two years without some radio based discussion taking place. However, at the recent Shell Seminar, held at Glenmore Lodge, the Rt. Hon. Michael Forsyth MP, announced that a dedicated F.M. frequency would soon become available to Mountain Rescue Teams. I had a call from Peter Cliff today, as I penned this, to say that at last a dedicated frequency on High Band F.M. has now been allocated. This is good news indeed, as this will greatly improve the all important aspect of radio communications for teams on rescues and training.

This is one of the classic cases which highlight the fact that politics sadly permeates Mountain Rescue at all levels. One might wish that a body of people in the main offering their voluntary services for the hopeful benefit of mountaineers and mountaineering in general would, somehow, be exempted from political wrangle. This regrettably is not the case. At one time running concurrently with, now following on from, the radios saga, Mountain Rescue is, at national level, faced with a very political issue of possible Search and Rescue helicopter service privatisation. This issue may not involve directly the rank and file team member. In the main these major issues are fielded by the Mountain Rescue Committee of Scotland — (a committee consisting mainly of team leaders, which does some sterling work) but such issues doubtless affect morale and attitudes towards commitment and the like among members.

As individuals we probably ask ourselves why we continue to be dragged from our families at all odd hours of the day or night, almost always in bad weather. I am sure all of us have different reasons for being involved in Mountain Rescue. In the Cairngorm Team our backgrounds in terms of workplace certainly vary very, very widely — doctors, dentists, teachers, outdoor education instructors, housewives, conservationists, electricians, foresters, oil industry workers, HM Forces personnel, policemen, apothecaries and engineers. Yet as a Team we continue to function efficiently and well, with seldom a cross word, appearing to be all of one mind in our commitment to Mountain Rescue. Much of the credit for the Team being the efficient smooth running machine that it is must go to individual members for their dedication and expertise, but obviously a great deal of the honour must go to our hard working Leader, Peter Cliff, who has dedicated hundreds of hours of his time and effort to make the Cairngorm Team what it is today — an organisation of which I am certainly very proud to be a minor part of.

APPENDIX 1

THE FINANCIAL PICTURE
By Martin Robertson

A summary of the expenditure and income has been extracted from the audited statements of accounts for the years 1963/4 to 1987/8. The financial year commences on 1st March and bank accounts were first opened on 5th March 1963 at the Bank of Scotland, Aviemore. Seven treasurers have been in office during the 25 year period, as follows:

1964, 1965	A. Lindsay
1966	A. Millar
1967	G. Andrew
1968-1973	T. Forbes
1974-1977	T.M. Robertson
1978-1986	J.C. Allen
1987-current	C. Barley

Successive treasurers and auditors have varied the presentation of the accounts, and every effort has been made in compiling the summary to achieve a uniform and consistent treatment of the figures. Several items require special mention, particularly with regard to equipment and vehicles where items have been acquired at reduced or even no cost, and consequently the amounts in the statements do not give the complete picture. The balance sheets do not give any indication of the value of the property, vehicles and equipment currently held, but it is estimated that the total is in excess of £50,000.

The following comments, read in conjunction with the summary, will hopefully give a more detailed account of the position.

A total of £782 was spent on equipment in the first two years, following the initial fund-raising campaign, which enabled a relatively modest amount to be purchased. Equipment was gradually improved until the 'Sponsored Walk' was discovered in 1973, and thereafter until the present day a much higher level of income and consequently expenditure has meant greatly improved and sophisticated items are now in use. For example, the team now operates with a total of 16 radios and 40 personal avalanche transceivers. The quality of the clothing, rucksacks and personal gear has been much enhanced. Boot allowances are included in this heading. It will be noted that in the most recent years purchases have exceeded £3,000 per annum. The team strength at present is 45 members.

Little expenditure was incurred on formal training courses in the early days, although Tommy Paul and Alastair McCook went to Norway. In recent years much more has been spent, and many members have benefitted from, for example, attendance at courses at Glenmore Lodge and elsewhere. This heading does not, of course, refer to the regular team training programme.

With regard to vehicles £40 is shown on the statement in 1973. This, in fact, refers to some minor expenses in connection with the handing-over ceremony of a Land Rover (the first vehicle), which was a donation from the Grants Whisky Company. The Ford and Land Rover Companies have also been generous, and the present position at May 1988 is that the team operates and maintains a Land Rover, Ford Transit van, Bedford van, Argocat, Terri All-terrain vehicle and trailer.

Having operated from Aviemore Police Station for many years the headquarters were transferred to Achantoul at the northern approach to Aviemore, and in 1983/4 expenditure of over £6,000 was incurred in erecting garages. A rental is paid to the Nature Conservancy Council for the use of the main building, which is also shared by the Meteorological Office.

Call-out expenses are travelling and other expenses (e.g. petrol and loss of wages) of team members attending rescue incidents and official training, and are subsequently reimbursed from the Police.

The main sources of income in the early years were the initial fund-raising campaign which produced a total of £1,036 in 1963/4 and regular fairly minor amounts from dances, collecting boxes and donations. From 1973 onwards sponsored walks have contributed largely to the overall healthy financial position. The first walk in 1973 to the Shelter Stone raised a total of £517, which seemed a large amount then; but subsequent walks through the Lairig Ghru have raised increasing amounts, the most recent in June 1987 making a profit of over £30,000. The Police make contributions in relation to members expenses, equipment, radios, insurance, road fund licences and property rental.

Year ended 28th February:	1964	1965	1966	1967	1868	1969	1970	1971	1972	19
EXPENDITURE:										
Administration	59	32	4	60	13	26	2	20	42	
Equipment	460	322	44	61	220	216	287	283	36	8
Training	114	38	45							
Vehicles — Acquisition										
Maintenance										
Property — Achantoul										
Call-out									6	4	
Other										
Total	633	392	93	121	233	242	289	309	82	10
INCOME										
Subscriptions				9	16	3	2			
Donations, Grants, etc.	871	139	108	57	114	50	165	27	138	13
Collection Boxes	23	22	33	20	13	10	22	4	16	
Dances, Raffles	134	203	133	140	81	85	83	46	114	1
Police Committee								50	50	50
Sponsored Walks										
Bank Interest	8	9	19	23	24	28	31	23	20	
Other										
Total	1036	373	293	249	248	176	353	150	338	158
Surplus/(Deficit)	403	(19)	200	128	15	(66)	64	(159)	256	5
Balance Carried Forward	403	384	584	712	727	661	725	566	822	14

RESCUE ASSOCIATION
OF ACCOUNTS

1974	1975	1976	1977	1978	1979	1980	1981	1982	1983	1984	1985	1986	1987	1988
96	62	215	139	150	190	162	246	136	99	191	215	224	328	214
625	1379	1454	1363	1389	1697	3362	2831	3087	2230	1794	3474	3897	3465	6689
14	14	46	74	396	140	517			1012	757	1529	1859	1878	1118
	40				560			4500			2764	6042		1250
	50	666	197	244	366	614	531	1378	1631	1295	1776	1925	4100	2134
										6095	424	203	1179	608
			95	282	199		533			1633	1377	1197	1430	1367
							320	187	233	588	349	333	330	333
735	1545	2381	1868	2461	3152	4655	4461	9288	5205	12353	11908	15680	12710	13713
10	10	4	5	4	7		10	10			5	6	9	5
473	206	1366	1207	1531	5558	796	336	1121	599	4042	5225	2874	3304	3167
71	15	206	106	60	247	48	47	110	20					64
276	133	74	93	7			323							
200			217	64	680	280	732	540	844	2015	2988	1159	2958	1823
517		1393		1594		4662		4976		14697		13264	259	31346
108	200	137	147	121	164	966	1071	895	353	374	972	1089	1262	1391
								165	362	156	568	287	112	484
655	564	3180	1775	3381	6656	6752	2519	7817	2178	21284	9758	18679	7904	38280
920	(981)	799	(93)	920	3504	2097	(1942)	(1471)	(3027)	8931	(2150)	2999	(4806)	24567
325	1344	2143	2050	2970	6474	8571	6629	5158	2131	11062	8912	11911	7105	31672

APPENDIX 2

LIST OF RESCUES

Compiled by Moira Snadden (Team Member since 1985)

The following is a summary of rescues carried out in the Cairngorm area from 1963-1987. From 1963-1970 detailed information has not been possible to obtain and in the earlier days rescues were often carried out by groups of volunteers rather than an "official" rescue team. There is little or no information available concerning man hours (mh) involved. From 1971-1981 only one time in man hours has been given. This time refers to C.M.R.T only.

1963
April 14th — Cairngorm Hillwalker (M40). Benighted.
September 15th — Coire Cas. Hillwalker (M23). Injuries.

1965
December 26th — Coire an t-Sneachda. Two climbers (M19 and 34) failed to return and a large search found one body on 27th December and the other on 8th January.

1966
April 9th — Lairig Ghru. T.A. on exercise. One man (32) collapsed with exhaustion near Pools of Dee; was put into a tent and sleeping bag until help arrived. Sleet and snow.
April 16th — Cairngorm Plateau. Youth (16) collapsed on summit of Macdhui from exhaustion. Weather conditions good.
July 26th — Feshie. Hillwalker (M) separated from companions near summit of Carn Ban Mor in mist. Took wrong turning and reached Glen Einich. Realised he was in wrong glen, climbed back up and descended into Glen Feshie. Walked out to Aviemore. No map or compass.
July 31st — Lairig Ghru. Youth (15) sprained ankle at Pools of Dee. Leader left injured lad with companion and went for help. Party well equipped.
September 17th — Cairngorms. Hillwalker (M18) set off to do the Four Tops. Failed to complete due to bad weather, dropped down to Glen Einich and became benighted. Returned safe and well the following morning. Search parties and helicopter.
December 8th — Lairig Ghru. Hillwalkers reached Sinclair hut from Aviemore but deteriorating weather turned them westwards. Became benighted. Found safe and well at 0900 hrs by C.M.R.T.

1967

February 28th — Strath Nethy. Glenmore Lodge party found two youths (21,19) suffering from exposure. Had climbed Cairngorm but taken wrong route on return. Taken to Nethy bothy and later evacuated. Blizzard conditions.

March 25th — Cairngorm Plateau. Youth (15) fell through cornice on Sputan Dearg. Injured arm and frostbite. Hillwalking with father. Very bad conditions.

April 20th — Cairngorm Plateau. Hillwalker (M30) overdue. Poor weather. No ice-axe, map or compass. Body found 8 days later near Braeriach. No injury. Search involved helicopters and dogs.

July 8th — Coire an t-Sneachda. Scout group leader (M27) left his party to descend from plateau by easy route while he abseiled down Aladdin's buttress. His body was later found at the foot of the buttress. Manilla or hemp rope and unconventional abseiling method.

July 11th — Braeriach. Hillwalker (M21) slipped on snow patch on eastern slopes. Compound leg fracture, multiple cuts and abrasions. From remains of air crash fashioned a splint and dragged himself out to Lairig Ghru. Found following morning.

August 12th — Cairngorm Plateau. Hillwalker (35) lost way on return from Macdhui to Cairngorm in mist. Descended to Lairig Ghru and returned following morning.

November 5th — Cairngorm Plateau. Hillwalker (M20) lost direction from Cairn Lochan to Car Park and drifted down to Loch Avon. Bad navigation in wind, mist and deep snow. Returned safe and well following morning.

December 27th — Coire an Lochain. Skier (M) slipped while climbing without ice axe or rope. Fatality.

December 28th — Cairngorm. Hillwalkers (F) found lost skier on plateau. Party benighted. Women well equipped. Skier with mild exposure.

1968

January 2nd — Cairngorm Plateau. Hillwalkers overdue but turned up late via Strath Nethy.

January 3rd — Cairngorm Plateau. Member of search party for above avalanched in Coire Raibert sustaining torn ankle ligaments. Helicoptered out.

July 5th — Cairngorm Plateau. Hillwalkers (M18,18,19) planning overnight route, became separated in mist. The one carrying the only compass met a man who guided him down. Rescue parties found rest of group next day in Sinclair hut — had gone up and down looking for lost companion.

July 22nd — Coire Etchachan. Climbers (M27,21) on Juniper Rib. Sling belay failed when leader fell 100ft. 2nd sustained fractured skull and ribs, leader bruised. No helmets.

August 5th — Cairngorm Plateau. Hillwalkers (M+F26) lost way in mist. Became benighted. Unable to navigate. Found safe and well following day by Sheiling.

August 25th — Cairngorm Plateau. Hillwalkers overdue on walk from Corrour to Cairngorm. Back safe early next morning.

December 18th — Cairngorm Plateau. Hillwalkers (M18,22+F20) overdue in bad weather. Spent night in refuge. Found next morning walking slowly over Cairngorm.

1969

February 1st — Coire an Lochain. Hillwalker (M21) set out for Jean's Hut. Failed to locate it and spent night in snow hole, his dog keeping him warm. Returned following morning.

February 19th — Coire Cas. A party on Glenmore Lodge survival course avalanched on headwall. Immediate help available, all safe soon after.

April 1st — Cairngorms. Youth (16) in training party collapsed on first day. Put into tent and rescued following morning.

July 13 — Cairngorm Plateau. Hillwalker (M19) lost map. Descended into Lairig Ghru and started up Braeriach thinking it was Ben Macdhui. Met hillwalker who directed him back into Lairig Ghru. He then turned south instead of north and came to Luibeg instead of Glenmore. Good weather.

August 13th — Cairngorms. Hillwalker (M20) overdue having underestimated the distance of planned route. Did not think anyone would worry. No map or compass.

August 15th — Etchachan hut. Hillwalker (F). Appendicitis at hut.

1970

March 6th — Coire an t-Sneachda. Hillwalkers (M21,31) tried to descend Aladdin's Couloir but found it too difficult. Lost way in poor weather through bad navigation and spent night in St Valery's refuge. Met search parties on their way down following morning.

May 9th — Feshie. Hillwalker (F55) drowned while crossing river Eidart holding hands with companions. Slipped and was swept into River Feshie. River running high. Bridge over river only a short distance upstream.

July 18th — Coire an Lochain. Hillwalker (M) slipped while scrambling. Head injuries. Wearing gymshoes.

July 19th — Braeriach. Hillwalkers lost on plateau. Benighted. Met search parties on way down.

December 28th — Coire na Ciste. Party of six hillwalkers left car park in late afternoon, reached Cairngorm summit then got lost in mist. Benighted in Coire na Ciste. Walked back following morning via Strath Nethy!

December 31st — Cairngorm Plateau. Skier overdue. Spent 14 hrs on plateau. Located by helicopter.

1971

March 13th — Coire an t-Sneachda. Climber (M28) fell sustaining fractured skull. Evacuation by helicopter.

April 4th — Creag Meagaidh. Climber fell on Centre Post, pulling off both seconds. Leader killed outright, both seconds sustaining serious injury. Carried down by C.M.R.T, Lochaber M.R.T. and Glenmore Lodge. 113mh.

September 10th — Coire an t-Sneachda. Hillwalker (F) cragfast in Goat Track/Red Gully area after becoming separated from her companions. C.M.R.T 21mh.

September 10th — Glen Feshie. Hillwalker (M), twisted knee on the Great Moss. C.M.R.T 26mh.

November 20th — Cairngorm Plateau. Group of six schoolchildren and two teachers overcome by bad weather in Lochan Buidhe area. The party spent two nights out on the plateau, 6 fatalities (1 teacher, 5 children). C.M.R.T 112mh.

1972

January 18th — Drumochter Pass. Evacuation of passengers trapped in their vehicles on snow blocked A9. C.M.R.T and Police 14mh.

February 13th — Coire an t-Sneachda. Party overdue from climbing in Red Gully. All night search in bad weather. Party turned up safe and well after night in Strath Nethy bothy. Started late, no map. C.M.R.T 60mh.

March 11th — Creag Meaghaidh. Climber (M) fell 500 ft in Easy Gully area sustaining severe head injuries, fractured ribs and legs. Wearing climbing helmet. C.M.R.T, Lochaber MRT, Glenmore Lodge and Police 111mh.

March 20th — Cannich. Two children reported missing after failing to meet up with father (a gamekeeper) on the moorland. Returned home unharmed. Team recalled en route. C.M.R.T 42mh.

May 16th — Inshriach. Search. Motorbike left by roadside for two days. Owner (M) returned unharmed. C.M.R.T 66mh.

August 28th — Loch Avon. Roped climber (M20) fell complete rope length on Shelter Stone crag, sustaining fatal injuries. Two lodge staff abseiled to casualty and effected two 300 ft lowers to foot of crag. Glenmore Lodge, C.M.R.T 203mh.

September 3rd — Braeriach. False alarm. Hillwalker reported abandoned rucksack on summit. On later arrival of team, rucksack had gone. C.M.R.T 96mh.

November 9th — Cairngorms. Hillwalker (F21) failed to return to Loch Morlich Youth Hostel after day walk. Weather deteriorated in the evening. After extensive search of area, helicopter found her unharmed by Fords of Avon bothy. Spent night out under a boulder. Lost map and no compass. RAF, C.M.R.T 125mh.

December 16th — Coire an t-Sneachda. Climbers (2M) reported missing, but turned up safe and well at midnight having walked out via Strath Nethy. No map or compass. Team on standby. S.A.R.D.A. and RAF.

December 27th — Cairngorm. Hillwalkers (2M,1F) reported missing after 4 day expedition. Night search. Reference in Sinclair bothy book located position in Jean's Hut. Safe and well. C.M.R.T 96mh.

December 29th — Northern Corries. Three students mistook Lochain for Sneachda when going on to plateau. Found on Saddle by RAF group. Safe and well. RAF, Glenmore Lodge and C.M.R.T 180mh.

1973

January 6th — Coire an Lochain. Climber (F21) fell over Great Slab, sustaining fatal injuries. Unroped, wearing climbing helmet. Glenmore Lodge and C.M.R.T. 90 mh.

January 13th — Coire an Lochain. Climber (F23) unroped slipped and fell out of Right Hand Branch of Y Gully sustaining serious injuries. Glenmore Lodge and C.M.R.T. 79mh.

January 22nd — Creag Dubh, Newtonmore. Climber (M25) fell, breaking both ankles. C.M.R.T. 18mh.

February 14th — Meall a Bhuachaille. False alarm. Red distress signals seen on a clear night. These turned out to be a lighthouse. C.M.R.T. 18mh.

March 26th — Coire an Lochain. Climber (M) fell in area. Evacuated by helicopter. C.M.R.T. 9mh.

July 2nd — Cairngorms. Night search for flares which turned out to be Skylab! Glenmore Lodge and C.M.R.T. 47mh.

July 4th — Cairngorm Plateau. Walker (M35) died on top of Sneachda. Heart attack. Evacuated by helicopter. Team on standby. C.M.R.T. 23mh.

September — Insh Marshes. Search for pony rider (F13). Found in the night. Safe and well.

October 21st — Lairig Ghru. Hillwalker (M) failed to arrive in Aviemore after setting out from Braemar in the morning. He took shelter in Corrour bothy and returned to Braemar by mid-day the following day. Braemar M.R.T. and C.M.R.T. 25mh.

October 28th — Creag Dubh, Newtonmore. Injured climber (broken ankle) evacuated from crag. RAF outdoor centre students and C.M.R.T. 15mh.

October 30th — Cairngorms. Four soldiers (M) overdue after day walk. Found the following morning, unharmed, near Nethy Bothy. Bad navigation. C.M.R.T. 79mh.

December 23rd — Coire an t-Sneachda. Hillwalkers (M20,24) avalanched in vicinity of Aladdin's Couloir. Slight injuries. Evacuated by helicopter. C.M.R.T. 27mh.

1974

March 17th — Coire Laogh Mor. Twelve members of a Mountain Centre avalanched. Two sustained head and ankle injuries. Stretchered out by Glenmore Lodge and C.M.R.T..

March 24th — Coire an Lochain. Climber (M20) fell 500 ft on descent when crampons balled up, breaking both legs. Stretcher evacuation.

April 7th — Coire an Lochain. Climbers (M24,23) hit by collapsing cornice and carried 200ft down slope, sustaining head and body injuries. Stretchered to Jean's Hut then helicoptered out.

May 29th — Lairig Ghru. Hillwalker (M35) became unwell on walk through Lairig Ghru. Helicopter evacuation.

June 12th — Coire na Ciste. Hillwalkers (F22,M30) fell sustaining broken pelvis and fractured ribs. Stretchered to Coire na Ciste car park.

June 21st — Lairig Ghru. Schoolboy became ill near Chalamain Gap. Stretcher evacuation.

July 20th — Lairig Ghru. Two boys in school party suffering from exposure. Put into tent. Helicopter evacuation.

August 11th — Lairig Ghru. Two tourists (F) reported missing. Turned up safe and well at Carbisdale Y.H. Helicopter, Braemar M.R.T., C.M.R.T.

November 3rd — Coire an Lochain. Climbers (M18,19) injured in Y Gully. Walked out unaided.

1975

January 27th — Coire an Lochain. Climber (M18) had completed The Vent when he appeared to fall back over edge. Fatal. Very bad conditions.

March 30th — Coire an Lochain. Climber (M) caught in avalanche below The Vent, sustaining severe leg injuries. High avalanche risk on all slopes. C.M.R.T. 31mh.

April 7th — Coire Cas. Cross-country skier (M51) found in Upper Cas area. Fatal. Severe northernly gales and whiteout conditions. C.M.R.T. 316mh.

August 3rd — Cairngorms. Two hillwalkers (1M and boy) overdue. They arrived at Etchachan bothy at 1830 hrs. The boy was left overnight with some M.B.A. members who were staying there. The man eventually arrived back on Speyside and returned for his son next day. No map and compass. This pair were the cause of another rescue incident some time previously. Team on standby.

November 2nd — Lairig Ghru. Hillwalker (M) overdue. Benighted in Corrour bothy. Found by helicopter. C.M.R.T. 24mh.

November 18th — Cairngorms. Two hillwalkers overdue from 4 day expedition. Found safe and well in Corrour bothy. Helicopter, C.M.R.T. 25mh.

December 20th — Cairngorms. Climber (F29) fell on ice in Coire an Lochain sustaining minor injuries. Unroped, wearing helmet. C.M.R.T. 22mh.

December 30th — Cairngorms. Party of four overdue from Etchachan via the Plateau. They turned up safe and well at Derry Lodge, having changed their plans due to atrocious weather conditions. Standby C.M.R.T. 1mh.

1976

December 31st 1975-January 1st 1976 — Cairngorm Plateau. Five hill-walkers overdue on walk from Ben Macdhui via Lairig Ghru to Avie-more. Arrived back safe and well. C.M.R.T. 18 mh.

January 3rd — Lairig Ghru. Hillwalkers (M50,F45) overdue. Delayed by severe weather, but found walking out the following morning, tired but well. C.M.R.T. 18 mh.

January 29th — Fiacaill of Coire Cas. Fatality (M25) on J.S.M.T.C. winter training. Benighted in emergency snow hole. Very severe gales and drifting snow, cause of death probably exposure. C.M.R.T. 18 mh.

February 14th — Coire an t-Sneachda. Climber (M) avalanched near base of Red Gully sustaining fatal injuries. Unroped, wearing helmet. C.M.R.T. 24 mh.

March 12th — Northern Corries. Party of Glenmore Lodge staff avalan-ched in Coire an Lochain en route to assist another Glenmore Lodge party avalanched on Goat Track in Sneachda. Seven casualties, one later dying of injuries. Helicopter evacuation. C.M.R.T. 56 mh.

March 13th — Coire an t-Sneachda. Fatality. Climber (M29) avalanched out of the upper slope of The Runnel, falling 140 ft. No runners but belay held. Helicopter evacuation. C.M.R.T. 32 mh.

June 10th — False alarm. Tourist reported hearing whistle in Fords of Avon area. Helicopter search revealed nothing. C.M.R.T. 27 mh.

September 8th-9th — Cairngorms. Seven Belgians (3M,4F) underestimated Cairngorm weather and conditions. Three were eventually stretchered out in difficult conditions, suffering from exposure. Poorly clad. C.M.R.T. 119 mh.

November 22nd — False alarm. Red flare and torchlight sighted on top of Coire na Ciste area. Search revealed nothing. C.M.R.T. 10 mh.

1977

January 11th — Loch Avon. Helicopter pilot had forced landing on the loch. No injuries. C.M.R.T. 120 mh.

January 12th — Cairngorm Plateau. Three hillwalkers (M20's) overdue on walk from Cairngorm to MacDhui. Walked in just as search was starting. Well equipped. C.M.R.T. 20mh.

January 29th — Creag Meagaidh. Climber (M) in Raeburn's Gully, slipped and fell 500 ft, sustaining slight injuries. Able to walk out with companions. C.M.R.T. 42 mh.

January 29th — Creag Meagaidh. Three Climbers (M) overdue from Stag Horn Gully. Returned safely at 9 pm. C.M.R.T. 1 mh.

March 12th — Cairngorms. Two skiers overdue from ski-ing round the Four Tops. Turned up safe and well at 0100 hrs. Delay due to icy conditions and broken torch. C.M.R.T. 2½mh.

March 29th — Cairngorm Plateau. Hillwalkers overdue on walk from Ben Macdhui to Strath Nethy. Returned safe and well. C.M.R.T. 2mh.

April 11th — Cairngorm Plateau. Hillwalker stepped through cornice on Cairn Lochan in white out, falling to the bottom. Walked out with cracked ribs. C.M.R.T. 9mh.

July 9th — Coire an t-Sneachda. Boy injured on Fiacaill ridge. Head and back injuries. Evacuation by helicopter. C.M.R.T. 7mh.

July 10th — Coire an Lochain. Climber (F) jammed finger in a crack on Savage Slit (two rings caused the jamming). Brute force won the day. Climber uninjured and able to walk out. Glenmore Lodge, C.M.R.T. 6mh.

July 17th — Lairig Ghru. Youth (16), suffering from blisters and fatigue, was left by his companions near the Sinclair Hut as he was walking too slowly. Did not make contact in Aviemore, but made his way home the following morning. C.M.R.T. 13mh.

August 10th — Cairngorm Plateau. Hillwalkers (father and son,16) became separated on walk from Etchachan bothy to Jean's Hut via Macdhui. Good weather. No map or compass. Later reunited by C.M.R.T. 4mh.

October 21st — Aviemore. Flare sighted on Craigellachie Crag. False alarm. C.M.R.T. 27mh.

October 23rd — Cairngorm Plateau. Two hillwalkers (M) separated on

Ben Macdhui when, in deteriorating weather, one decided to return to dumped camping gear at Garbh Uisge Beag. He did not see his companion again and reported him overdue. Turned up safe and well following morning after being looked after by a party who were in the Shelter Stone. C.M.R.T. 3mh.

December 11th — Creag Meagaidh. Hillwalkers (father and son,10) overdue. Became benighted in white out conditions. Found safe and well by helicopter. S.A.R.D.A. 22mh, C.M.R.T. 118mh.

December 28th — Coire an Lochain. Climber (M20's) avalanched while climbing up to The Vent. Leg injuries. C.M.R.T. 139mh.

December 27/28th — Cairngorms. Two climbers failed to return after finishing climbing in Coire an t-Sneachda. Poor conditions. Descended Coire Raibert to Loch Avon. No map or compass. Found by helicopter following day at Fords of Avon. C.M.R.T. 139mh.

1978

January 4th — Coire an t-Sneachda. Climbers overdue. Set out too late and underestimated weather conditions. C.M.R.T. 12mh.

January 4th — Lairig Ghru. Hillwalker (M30's) overdue. He had descended the March Burn, his companion deciding that it was too steep and turning back. Underestimated time and energy required to complete route. Weather conditions poor, drifting snow and strong wind. Found tired but well in Sinclair hut. S.A.R.D.A., C.M.R.T. 20mh.

January 11th — Ghillie (M23) overdue on walk from Braemar to Feshie. Lightly clad, succumbed to severe weather and cold. Helicopter located body. S.A.R.D.A., C.M.R.T. 55mh.

January 14th — Coire an Lochain. False alarm. Cries for help reported from Vent area. Helicopter, Glenmore Lodge, C.M.R.T. 65mh.

January 21st — Coire an t-Sneachda. Four climbers injured in two separate avalanche incidents. Two head injuries, one knee and one exposure case. Severe weather. C.M.R.T. 38mh.

January 23rd — Creag Meagaidh. Hillwalkers (M20's) overdue. No map. Arrived safe and well next morning in Glen Roy after overnight bivouac. Helicopter, Glenmore Lodge, Tulloch, I.M.C., C.M.R.T. 195mh.

January 28/29th — Creag Meagaidh. Hillwalker (M20's) left exhausted in bivouac by companions on Coire Ardair track. Weather too severe for evacuation. Rescued following day by Helicopter from Fort William. Lochaber M.R.T., C.M.R.T. 27mh.

January 28th — Cairngorms. Student (M) overcome by exhaustion en route from Faindouran bothy to Glenmore. Severe conditions. Helicopter evacuation. C.M.R.T. 6mh.

January 31st — Slochd, A9. Police request to probe snowdrifts. Nothing found. C.M.R.T. 104mh.

March 24th — Coire Cas. Climber (M) fell through cornice on headwall walking from Coire an t-Sneachda to car park. Minor injuries, walked out unaided. White out. C.M.R.T. 26mh.

March 24/25th — Ben Alder. Two youths (14) suffering exposure, one severe, while walking from Corrour station to bothy. Taken to Benalder Cottage by passing walkers. Severe weather conditions, poorly equipped. Taken out by boat. C.M.R.T. 16mh.

March 25th — Loch Avon. Climber injured knee, bivouacked at Shelter Stone. Severe weather conditions. Helicopter evacuation. C.M.R.T. 27mh.

April 1st/2nd — Creag Meagaidh. Hillwalkers fell over cliff in whiteout. No injuries, spent night in snowhole. C.M.R.T. 221mh.

April 9th — Cairngorm Plateau. Party of six hillwalkers overdue on walk from Macdhui to car park. Found by Helicopter next day in Strath Nethy having got lost. C.M.R.T. 30mh.

April 10th — Aviemore. Walker overdue from Craigellachie nature trail. False alarm. C.M.R.T. 18mh.

July 4th — Lairig Ghru. School party suffering from exposure. Dealt with by Braemar M.R.T., C.M.R.T. assistance at control unit. C.M.R.T. 3mh.

August 20th — Braeriach. Hillwalkers became separated in poor visibility. Arrived safely. Team on standby. C.M.R.T. 3mh.

August 30th — Cairngorms. Hillwalkers overdue from traverse of Four Tops. Arrived safely after midnight. No compass. Team on standby. C.M.R.T. 2mh.

October 16th — Braeriach. Flare reported. False alarm. C.M.R.T. 23mh.

December 26th — Einich. Avalanche in Coire Bogha-cloiche. Two fatalities. Blizzard conditions. S.A.R.D.A., C.M.R.T. 89mh.

1979

January 1st — Cairngorms. Ski tourers (M25,19) underestimated time for trip to Cairngorm and Macdhui. Returned at 2300 hrs. Standby, C.M.R.T. 2mh.

January 27th — Coire an t-Sneachda. Climber (M) soloing fell at cornice in Crotched Gully. Fractured both ankles and severe lacerations. Helicopter evacuation. C.M.R.T. 9 mh.

January 29th — Cairngorms. Climber (M) returned on 28th to Jean's Hut to collect food left during his friend's accident previous day. Went onto plateau to retrieve rucksack and camera but got lost in whiteout. Found next day at Loch Etchachan having survived night out with no gear. Blizzard conditions. Rucksack found by walkers on day of friends accident and taken to police station. Glenmore Lodge, C.M.R.T. 100mh.

February 18/19th — Drumochter Pass, A9. Police requested help to search abandoned cars and drifts in terrible conditions. No casualties. C.M.R.T. 65mh.

March 3rd — Coire an t-Sneachda. Climber fell on Goat Track. C.M.R.T. 24mh.

March 13th — Cairngorms. Standby. Party overdue, but arrived later. C.M.R.T. 2mh.

April 18th — Cairngorm. Hillwalkers (family with two children) overdue. Found at top chairlift station, cold but unharmed. Soft, deep snow underfoot. Mother and children inadequately clad. C.M.R.T. 60mh.

August 18th — Abernethy. Old lady overdue from afternoon walk. Probably fell asleep! Unharmed. C.M.R.T. 12mh.

December 16-24th — Coire an t-Sneachda. Hillwalker became separated from companions at top of the Goat Track. Weather conditions terrible throughout search. Body found five days later on the cornice above The Runnel. Glenmore Lodge, Lochaber M.R.T., S.A.R.D.A., RAF Kinloss, Leuchars. C.M.R.T. 312mh.

December 31st — Lairig Ghru. Climbers (M) got lost after climbing in Coire an Lochain. Avalanched into Lairig Ghru sustaining minor injuries. Picked up following day by Helicopter. C.M.R.T. 5mh.

1980

January 8th — Coire an t-Sneachda. Climbers (M30's) overdue from Red Gully. Underestimated time and weather conditions. Benighted at top of gully, but walked out next morning. C.M.R.T. 100mh.

January 17th — Coire Laogh Mor. Partial assistance given to exhausted cadet. C.M.R.T. 3mh.

March 3rd — Braeriach. Cross-country skier overdue (M30's) located following day in Lairig Ghru. No injury. Helicopter. S.A.R.D.A.. C.M.R.T. 162mh.

March 29/30th — Cairngorms. Skiers (M,F) failed to locate Ptarmigan ski tow in whiteout conditions. Wandered about all night and finally ended up in Strath Nethy. Found safe and well next morning. Wearing downhill ski gear. S.A.R.D.A., C.M.R.T. 99mh.

May 17th — Lairig Ghru. Hillwalker (M66) overdue. Became tired and spent night in Corrour bothy. Helicopter located him following morning. C.M.R.T. 28mh.

June 27th — Glen Feshie. Overdue Glider. Found S. of Corrour next morning safe and well. He had been over-ambitious in a strong wind. C.M.R.T. 80mh.

August 8th — Kingussie crag. Climber (M19) slipped dislocating knee. C.M.R.T. 12mh.

December 30th — Lairig Ghru. Hillwalker (M20's) died of exhaustion and exposure in Cairngorm blizzard. Was wearing pacemaker. C.M.R.T. 121mh.

1981

January 27th — Cairngorms. False alarm. Flare sighted on clear night. C.M.R.T. 32mh.

September 20th — Glen Feshie. Hillwalker (M33) overdue. Unable to cross a swollen stream, so put up tent and waited until the next day for the streams to subside. Braemar M.R.T., C.M.R.T. 18mh.

September 27th — Lairig Ghru. Young girl (16) with Venture Scouts on walk from Blair Atholl to Aviemore. Reached Corrour bothy suffering from exposure, apparently recovered, and carried on next day. Suffered again. Evacuated by helicopter from Sinclair Hut. Inadequate clothing. C.M.R.T. 30mh.

September 28th — Feshie woods. Experienced glider pilot crashed, possibly due to broken wing. Fatality. C.M.R.T. 90mh.

December 23rd — Strath Nethy. False alarm. Flare sighted on cold clear night. C.M.R.T. 7mh.

December 30/31st — Cairngorms. Party of five climbers (M) went to climb Escalator on Hell's Lum. One soloed and reached top. By 2100 hrs, no sign of others so put down top rope and went for help. Three later reached top using top rope, and decided to bivouac. One was blown over the top in his bivi bag, falling 900 ft without sustaining serious injuries. He was later flown out by Helicopter. The other climber was found dead on the crag. Strong winds, poor visibility, late starting route. RAF Kinloss, Glenmore Lodge, S.A.R.D.A., C.M.R.T. 180mh.

1982

January 18th/21st — Beinn a'Ghlo, Tilt. Hillwalker (M41) avalanched on north slopes. Had been away from home since 13th, intending to return on 17th. Fatality. Braemar M.R.T., Glenmore Lodge, S.A.R.D.A., RAF Leuchars and Kinloss, police and civilian volunteers, C.M.R.T. 331mh.

April 8th — Braeriach. Hillwalker (M42) lost on Sron na Lairig. Severe weather, no compass or ice axe. Found safe and well following morning. Helicopter, Glenmore Lodge, S.A.R.D.A., C.M.R.T. 88mh.

October 4/5th — Lairig Ghru. Hillwalker (M59) overdue. Found safe and well in Sinclair bothy. Had been unable to cross burn. Braemar M.R.T., C.M.R.T. 18mh.

October 9th — Cairngorms. Hillwalker (M22) slipped while descending Lurcher's crag. Fractured skull and spine. Helicopter evacuation at night. Glenmore Lodge, C.M.R.T. 72mh.

December 22/23rd — Cairngorm Plateau. Two youths (M18) became benighted after misjudging time to walk from car park to Loch Avon and back. Left car park at midday. Spent night in snow hole in Coire Raibert. Found following morning, one suffering from severe exposure. Calm night, poor equipment. Glenmore Lodge, S.A.R.D.A., C.M.R.T. 66mh.

December 31st — Braeriach. Hillwalker (M24) slipped while descending south flank of Braeriach, sustaining fatal injuries. Helicopter evacuation. Glenmore Lodge 16mh, C.M.R.T. 51mh.

1983

January 2nd — Fiacaill Coire an t-Sneachda. Hillwalker (M20) dislocated knee after being blown over in gale. Doctor failed to reduce dislocation so airlifted to hospital. Glenmore Lodge 2½mh, C.M.R.T. 1½mh.

January 6th — Cairngorms. Hillwalkers (M, both 18) got into difficulties descending into Lairig Ghru from Macdhui. Snowholed. Next day, one slipped, but both managed to reach Sinclair Hut. Well equipped. Minor injuries, frostbite. Helicopter evacuation. Glenmore Lodge 3½mh, C.M.R.T. 4½mh.

February 21st — Coire an Lochain. Climbers (M28) in difficulties on Daydream. Leader fell from cornice (slip/windslab?). No runners. Fractured femur. Second cragfast. Cliff lower, Helicopter evacuation. Glenmore Lodge 26mh, C.M.R.T. 130mh.

March 29th — Dulnain Bridge village. Girl (6) drowned in River Dulnain. Helicopter, local volunteers. S.A.R.D.A., C.M.R.T. 94mh.

April 2/3rd — Bynack More. Hillwalker (M35) benighted at head of Water of Caiplich. Map had blown away. Whiteout conditions. Well equipped. Found by Helicopter following morning. Glenmore Lodge 7mh, S.A.R.D.A. 18mh, C.M.R.T. 46mh.

April 23/25th — Kintail. Three hillwalkers set out to walk Five Sisters ridge. Two turned back in deteriorating weather, one carried on alone but was reported overdue. Found two days later at base of steep cliffs. Fatal. Slipped on steep grass and rocks. C.M.R.T., Kinloss, Kintail, Leuchars, Glenelg, Lochaber & Skye M.R.T., S.A.R.D.A. over 1,000mh for all Teams.

May 14th — Creag Dubh, Newtonmore. Climber (M20's) fell during training exercise (RAF), sustaining serious injuries. Roped. Helicopter, Glenmore Lodge 7mh, C.M.R.T. 10mh.

May 22nd — Strath Nethy. Hillwalker F62) sprained ankle near Bynack stable. Helicopter evacuation. Glenmore Lodge 2mh, C.M.R.T. 4mh.

May 28/29th — Lairig Ghru. Hillwalker (M62) collapsed from exhaustion at Pools of Dee. Bivouaced with help from passing walker. Evacuation by stretcher to Sinclair hut, then tracked vehicle. Poorly equipped. Glenmore Lodge 35mh, C.M.R.T. 100mh.

September 20th — River Beauly. Suspected suicide (M). Body recovered by C.M.R.T. 70mh.

December 18th — Braeriach. Hillwalker (M21) separated from companion in poor weather. Companion retreated to Sinclair Hut and raised alarm. The other, with no map or torch, went on to Braeriach and then returned to the Sinclair. C.M.R.T. 4mh.

1984

January 1st — Coire an t-Sneachda. Climbers (M20,22) failed to navigate out after late start on Aladdin's Mirror. Climbed slowly, one inexperienced, in deteriorating weather. Benighted at top of Fiacaill a Coire Cas. Good bivouac gear. Found next morning. Helicopter, Glenmore Lodge 12mh, S.A.R.D.A. 25mh, RAF Kinloss 90mh, C.M.R.T. 108mh.

January 5/6th — Coire an t-Sneachda. Spanish climber (M24), said to be experienced, soloed in coire then got lost walking out. Found in Strath Nethy near Bynack stable. No map or compass. Helicopter, Glenmore Lodge 30mh, RAF Kinloss 120mh, S.A.R.D.A. 20mh, C.M.R.T. 84mh.

January 6/7th — Cairngorms. Poorly clad member of Mendips Rescue Team (M33), set off up Lairig Ghru in the afternoon. He read the word "good" off the board describing the ski runs and took this as a weather forecast. Walked up Lairig Ghru, up March Burn, down to Loch Avon (he thought this was Coire an Lochain) and ended up in Tomintoul. 45km walk. No rucksack, map, compass or food. Helicopter, Glenmore Lodge 12mh, S.A.R.D.A. 10mh, C.M.R.T. 108mh.

January 15/16th — Coire an Lochain. Party of six school pupils and one teacher benighted when they failed to navigate back to Jean's hut after climbing The Couloir. Rucksacks had been left in hut. Ended up in Strath Nethy and stayed overnight in Bynack stable. Walked out to Glenmore Lodge next morning. Weather reasonable. Helicopter, RAF Kinloss 75mh, Glenmore Lodge 44mh, C.M.R.T. 45mh.

January 21st — Assistance given to farm worker with broken leg as ambulance couldn't reach casualty because the road was blocked by snow. C.M.R.T. 8mh.

January 20/22nd — Coire an Lochain. Hillwalkers (M21,22,24,21) failed to locate Jean's hut on 21st so camped. Weather deteriorated on 22nd and tent blew away. Decided to walk out but one by one, three died of exposure in terrible weather. The fourth walked out on morning of 22nd, exhausted. Wind gusting to 90mph. Helicopter, RAF Kinloss & Leuchars, S.A.R.D.A., Glenmore Lodge. 300mh all Teams.

January 21/22nd — Drumochter. About 450 people trapped in cars on A9 at Drumochter Pass due to snowdrifts. Assisted them either to Drumochter Lodge or Dalwhinnie. C.M.R.T. 171mh.

January 23/24th — Cairngorms. Instructor (M29) and student (M36) from J.S.M.T.C. intended to snowhole in Feidh Buidhe on 20th, then spend 21st at Shelter Stone. Searching began 23rd in very bad weather with high avalanche risk. Found on 26th on rim of Coire an t-Sneachda by J.S.M.T.C. Fatal, succumbed to hypothermia. Helicopters, S.A.R.D.A., Glenmore Lodge 50mh, RAF Kinloss & Leuchars 1440mh, C.M.R.T. 480mh.

February 19th — Coire an t-Sneachda. Hillwalker (M23) scrambling up mixed snow and rock of Fiacaill of Coire an t-Sneachda. Stopped to put on crampons but blown off ridge sustaining fatal injuries. Helicopter, Glenmore Lodge. C.M.R.T. on standby.

March 2/3rd — Bynack More. Hillwalker (M18), on training exercise (RAF), became separated from companions. Got into sleeping bag and orange polybag and promptly slid off downhill. Stayed put, failed to attract rescuers attention later in night when they passed close by, since whistle and torch were up the hill with rucksack. Found next morning by Helicopter. Glenmore Lodge 40mh, S.A.R.D.A. 50mh, C.M.R.T. 270mh.

March 26/27th — Glen Feshie. Hillwalker (M22) overdue. Extensive search of avalanche debris with threat of further avalanche. Body found in May in Coire Domhain avalanche tip. Helicopter, RAF Kinloss & Leuchars 620mh, S.A.R.D.A. 34mh, C.M.R.T. 155mh.

June 3rd — Cairngorm Plateau. Tourist (F45) overdue on walk in Coire Cas. Found on Cairngorm summit late at night. Cold and tired. Walked down to cloud base, then helicoptered out. S.A.R.D.A. 38mh, Glenmore Lodge 4mh, C.M.R.T. 3mh.

August 23rd — Cairngorm Plateau. Hillwalkers (mother and two sons) became separated. Son turned up later safe and well. Good weather. C.M.R.T. on standby.

August 26th — Cairngorms. Hillwalker (M27) went for walk on 18th with large rucksack. Helicopter search made on 25th, team search of area on 26th. He reported to police down South on September 9th. C.M.R.T. 188mh.

September 3rd — Lairig Ghru. False alarm. Hillwalker (M) left route card with Aviemore police. Failed to tell Braemar police that he had arrived. C.M.R.T. 12mh.

November 13th — Glen Feshie. False alarm. Hillwalkers (M) reported overdue by wife who had got her dates muddled. Found camping in glen. Helicopter, Glenmore Lodge 2½mh, C.M.R.T. 53mh.

November 19/21st — Mail plane on routine flight crashed into hillside killing pilot. 2 Helicopters, RAF Leuchars & Kinloss, S.A.R.D.A., C.M.R.T. 380mh.

December 27th — Coire an t-Sneachda. Leader (M30) fell off top pitch of Spiral Gully. No runners. Pulled off second (M41) belayed to inadequately placed deadman. Both then fell 300 ft. Second killed outright (wearing helmet), leader sustained superficial injuries (no helmet). Helicopter, Glenmore Lodge 7mh, C.M.R.T. 7mh.

1985

February 19th — Lairig Ghru. Three hillwalkers lost in area of Jean's Hut and Sinclair Hut. Had left their equipment in Jean's Hut. Spent night in Sinclair. Glenmore Lodge 2mh, C.M.R.T. 4mh.

March 31st — Lairig Ghru. Hillwalkers (M19,F20) got lost going S. to N. through Lairig Ghru. Found Garbh Coire bothy, thinking it to be Sinclair Hut. Looked after by occupants of bothy and found next day by Braemar M.R.T. Helicopter evacuation. C.M.R.T. 56mh, Braemar M.R.T. 150mh.

June 22nd — Craigellachie Crag, Aviemore. Tourist (M22) found dead at bottom of crag. Possibly slipped on steep wet grass while bird watching. Short stretcher lower and carry. C.M.R.T. 8mh.

June 27th — Grantown Woods. Attempted suicide (F23). C.M.R.T. organised search. Found by S.A.R.D.A. dog, just alive. S.A.R.D.A., C.M.R.T.

July 20th — Creag Dubh, Newtonmore. Climber (M20) fell, while helping to rescue a cragfast boy (10), sustaining head injuries. Boy said he could make his own way back from top of crag, but must have fallen. Found at bottom of crag with broken leg. Helicopter evacuation. C.M.R.T. 35mh.

September 1/2nd — Lairig Ghru. Hillwalker (M63) collapsed through exhaustion at Pools of Dee. Two companions stayed with him while two others went for help. Team helped him down to Sinclair and then evacuated by track vehicle. C.M.R.T. 135mh.

October 5/6th — Braeriach. Services party of seven and school party of 23 both overdue. All turned up safe and well. S.A.R.D.A. 7½mh, C.M.R.T. 52mh.

December 31st — Coire Cas. Hillwalker (M24) went back to headwall to retrieve an ice hammer lost previous day while glissading. Caught by avalanche. Death by asphyxia. Wearing Pieps. S.A.R.D.A. 10mh, Glenmore Lodge 20mh, C.M.R.T. 100mh.

1986

January 5/6th — Hell's Lum, Loch Avon. Two climbers benighted on Deep Cut Chimney. Left sacs at bottom and were too slow on route. Benighted. Bad forecast but luckily weather moderated after 0100hrs. Helicopter evacuation. S.A.R.D.A. 9mh, C.M.R.T. 114mh.

January 11th — Coire an t-Sneachda. Hillwalker (M39) slipped and fell 200 ft from W. ridge of Coire an t-Sneachda. Suspected spinal fracture. Glenmore Lodge 54mh, C.M.R.T. 112mh.

March 6th — Ben Macdhui. Hillwalker (M50) overdue. Found in Lairig Ghru having fallen from W. slopes of Cairn Lochan. Very windy — possibly blown off his feet. Fatal. Found by Helicopter. RAF Kinloss & Leuchars 320mh, Glenmore Lodge 90mh, S.A.R.D.A., C.M.R.T. 200mh.

March 20/21st — Cairngorms. Series of incidents caused by hurricane winds — 156mph — recorded before anemometer broke. Three Glenmore Lodge parties on S.M.L.T.B. assessment got into difficulties:

1. Student went missing from snow hole. Instructor searching for him was avalanched breaking his ankle.

2. Another instructor either fell over or was blown over cornice onto steep ground which avalanched. Unable to rejoin students, who made their own way to Derry Lodge.

3. Another assessment party out of radio contact for a long time — walked out via Strath Nethy to Glenmore Lodge.

By next morning weather had moderated enough for helicopter to airlift off all on Cairngorm Plateau. Braemar M.R.T. 30mh, Glenmore Lodge 64mh, RAF Kinloss & Leuchars 40mh, C.M.R.T. 40mh.

April 2/3rd — Cairngorms. Poorly clad, partially-sighted, hillwalker (M32) lost way in whiteout. Found at Corrour by Braemar M.R.T.. C.M.R.T. 128mh, Glenmore Lodge 27mh, Braemar M.R.T. 16mh.

July 19th — Ben Macdhui. Hillwalker left wife and son on N. top of Macdhui in 50 yd visibility, while he went on to true summit. The other two were tired. He was the only one with map and compass and he did not find them again. They were found by Helicopter well off route. Glenmore Lodge 2mh, C.M.R.T. 24mh.

July 24th — Braeriach. Hillwalker (M42) separated from companion. One returned to raise the alarm, the other turned up after midnight. Glenmore Lodge 3mh, C.M.R.T. 10mh.

September 2nd — Lairig Ghru. Cyclist (M30) became exhausted and separated from companions who did not wait for him. Found by climbers who looked after him in the Sinclair Hut. Located by search party around 0300hrs. S.A.R.D.A. 4mh, C.M.R.T. 12mh.

September 28th — Fiacaill of Coire Cas. Hillwalker (F16) on mountain course stumbled near top of Fiacaill T-bar. C.M.R.T. party on training exercise nearby was able to give assistance. Suspected broken ankle. C.M.R.T. 12mh.

November 1st — Coire Cas. Hillwalker (F18) collapsed on Fiacaill of Coire Cas. Unconscious initially, later became delirious. Stretchered to car park. Cairngorm Chairlift Company 4mh, C.M.R.T. 4mh.

December 12th — Craigellachie, Aviemore. Tourists (M22,22) became cragfast. C.M.R.T. climbed up to casualties, roped them up and took them to top of cliff. Led off to roadside. Both suffering from exposure. C.M.R.T. 6mh.

December 23rd — Cairngorm. Piste Skier overdue. Failed to meet companions, sheltered behind hut and so was missed by ski patrol. Walked down and found an open hut. S.A.R.D.A. 2mh, C.M.R.T. 64mh.

1987

February 20th — Strath Nethy. Hillwalkers benighted due to poor navigation. Walked out next day. C.M.R.T. 2mh.

February 22nd — Cairngorm Plateau. Skiers (M40,34) became benighted on return from Macdhui when ski binding gave problems and one skin came off. Found a snowhole in Coire Raibert. Helicoper, S.A.R.D.A., Tweed Valley 77mh, C.M.R.T. 126mh.

March 3/4th — Gael Charn. Hillwalkers (M50's, F40's) avalanched. One died outright, the other went for help but died of exposure/exhaustion on the way. Very stormy day with stong winds. RAF Kinloss M.R.T. 82mh, S.A.R.D.A., C.M.R.T. 165mh.

March 13th — Braeriach. Climbers (M35,36). Second failed to follow leader over cornice. Leader left him at 1400hrs and only reported to police at 1100hrs next day having stopped for a sleep on the way! Second was wet and cold when rescued from top of climb by helicopter. C.M.R.T. 4mh.

March 14th — Creag Meagaidh. Cornice collapsed above Staghorn Gully dislodging two climbers. Held by 3rd. Fatality. Possible skull fracture. Helicopter evacuation. Lochaber M.R.T. 24mh, C.M.R.T. 26mh.

April 5th — Cairngorm Plateau. Four hillwalkers (M) benighted due to poor weather and bad navigation. Helicopter evacuation. Glenmore Lodge 6mh, C.M.R.T. 32mh.

April 19th — Huntly's cave. Climber (M26) fell about 30 ft, pulling out runners, and hitting the ground. Broken leg. C.M.R.T. 9mh.

May 5th — Lairig Ghru. Hillwalker (M38), suffering from exhaustion at Pools of Dee, was helped to Sinclair Hut by companions. Stretchered out some hours later. Strong wind and snow showers. C.M.R.T. 100mh.

May 19/20th. Glen Strathfarrar. Hillwalker (M64) overdue from walk up An Riabhachan. Got lost and became benighted. Walked out next morning. Helicopter, RAF Kinloss M.R.T. 40mh, C.M.R.T. 100mh.

May 20th — Feshie. Hillwalker (M59) slipped on rocks in Corie Garblach breaking leg. Helicopter evacuation. C.M.R.T. 8mh.

May 23rd — Creag Dubh, Newtonmore. Climber (M) fell off 1st pitch of Acapulco, pulling out runners. Chest injury. Helicopter evacuation. C.M.R.T. 6mh.

May 28th — Inverness. Patient (M34) of Dunain Hospital absconded. Forest search. Found dead on May 30th. Helicopter, I.M.C. 48mh, RAF Kinloss 60mh, C.M.R.T. 110mh.

July 29th — Cairngorms. Group of six (16-18 yrs) on Duke of Edinburgh assessment got lost twice but later walked out to Braemar. Bad navigation. C.M.R.T. 14mh, Braemar M.R.T.

August 31st/September 1st — Cairngorms. Two Venture Scouts (M17) got lost in Feshie area, crossing Geldie burn onto S. side, thereby moving out of region covered by their only map. Found unharmed by helicopter late following day. S.A.R.D.A., Braemar M.R.T. 52mh, Aberdeen 340mh, RAF Kinloss & Leuchars M.R.T. 540mh, C.M.R.T. 353mh.

November 8th — Rothiemurchus woods. Missing walker (diabetic). Found safe but confused. S.A.R.D.A. 36mh, C.M.R.T. 138mh.

November 14/15th — Cairngorm. Hillwalker (M28) overdue. Found next day at base of Stac An Faradh. Exposure, spinal fracture. Fatal. Helicopter evacuation. RAF Kinloss & Leuchars M.R.T. 392mh, S.A.R.D.A. 32mh, C.M.R.T. 245mh.

TEAM LEADERS 1963-88

Tommy Paul 1963-4

Peter Bruce 1964-9

Alistair McCook 1969-72

Molly Porter 1972-81

Peter Cliff 1981-

APPENDIX 3

LIST OF TEAM MEMBERS 1963-1988

(Compiled by Helen Ross, and with apologies for any omissions)

Hon. Presidents: Duncan Grant, Alistair McCook.

Hon. Vice-President: Jack Thomson.

Chairmen		Team Leaders	
Dr T.W. Palmer	1963-1965	Tommy Paul	1963-1964
Duncan Grant	1965-1967	Peter Bruce	1964-1969
Dr Neil MacDonald	1967-1970	Alistair McCook	1969-1972
Jack Thomson	1970-1973	Molly Porter	1972-1981
Dr Neil MacDonald	1974-1977	Peter Cliff	1981-
Martin Robertson	1977-1980		
John Allen	1980-1983		
Chris Barley	1983-1986		
David Craig	1986-		

Team Members

Allan, Frank	Bonnington, Craig	Crombie, John
Allan, Sandy	Broadhead, Dave	Crompton, Jim
Allan (nee Dr Janis Tait)	Brough, Colin	Cummings, Dave
Allen, John	Brown, Marjory	Dallas, John
Anderson, Willie	Bruce, Peter	Dean, C.
Ankorne, Paul	Bulmer, Digby	Dennis, Roy
Armstrong, Stuart	Burley, Bins	Douglas, R.
Atkinson, Sarah	Burns, John	Drew, Dan
Auld, Graham	Cain, Alistair	Duggleby, Tim
Bantick, Allan	Cameron, D.	Dwyer, Gerry
Barclay, Bruce	Carter, Andrew	Faulkner, Jeff
Barley, Chris	Chadwick, Steve	Ferguson, Charlie
Barley, Denise	Clark, Jimmy	Ferguson, Peter
Barron, Hugh	Clarke, Graham	Finlayson, Peter
Bell, Alan	Cliff, Peter	Fleming, J.
Benton, Jane	Cowan, Dr Leslie	Forwood, Nick
Black, Donnie	Craig, Dave	Fraser, Morton
Blackwood, Lyall	Crayk, Fred	Fursman, Dick

Gaff, Roger
Gair, Colin
Geddes, Helen
Golding, Peter
Gould, John
Grant, Alistair
Grant, Jim
Grant, Dr Peter
Gray, Dr Duncan
Gray, Paul
Grossett, James
Hall, John
Henderson, G.
Hetherington, Scott
Hinde, John
Hinde, Tony
Howie, Dr Graham
Hudson, Iain
Jack, Nick
Jamieson, Harry
Jardine, Sue
Jarvie, Bob
Jervis, J.
Jones, Tom
Kemley, Dick
Kerr, Bill
Kerr, Jim
Kerr, Moira
King, John
Kinnaird, Bob
Laird, S.
Lawther, Eric
Liddell, Walter
Lindsay, Kenny
Lindsay, Sandy
Little, P.
Lyall, John
MacBeath, R.
McCook, Alistair
MacDonald, J.
MacDonald, Leslie
MacDonald, Dr Neil

McHardy, Richard
MacKenzie, Alan
MacKenzie, Tommy
MacKenzie, Billy
MacLean, John
MacLeod, C.
McNeish, Stewart
MacPherson, Willie
MacRae, J.
McVean, Donald
Mackie, Barney
Mackie (nee Wellwood), Julie
Mardon, Philip
Marks, Bill
Marshall, Hamish
Mather, Sarah
McHardy, Richard
Meikle, David
Miller, Andrew
Millward, Neil
Morris, David
Munro, Dr David
Ormerod, P.
Parish, G.
Patchett, John
Paton, George
Paul, Tommy
Paxton, James
Payne, Malcolm
Pierce, Dave
Pimm, Rod
Pirie, Eric
Porter, Jo
Porter, Molly
Pott, J.
Rennie, Paul
Reynard, B.
Robertson, Martin
Rosenfield, Dennis
Ross, Helen
Ross, Ian
Ross, M.

Ross, Paul
Saunders, Frank
Scarbrough, George
Scarbrough (now Wells), Pat
Sclater, Malcolm
Sharp, D.
Shaw, Sandy
Simond, P.
Smith, Andy
Smith, Iain
Smith, Ian
Smith, T.
Smith, William
Smyth, Paddy
Snadden, Dr David
Snadden, Moira
Spalding, Steve
Sparks, Nigel
Sterritt, Wes
Stevens, Tony
Stevens, Simon
Stewart, Gordon
Stokes, Rodney
Stuart, Chris
Sutherland, Alex

Sutton, Alistair
Tait (Allan), Dr Janis
Taplin, D.
Taplin, R.
Taylor, Ken
Taylor, Newby
Thomas, Pat
Thomson, Chris
Thomson, Jack
Todd, Willie
Travers, Harry
Travers, Steve
Treadwell, Ray
Utton, Richard
Wakeling, Ann
Watters, D.
Webster, Dick
Weir, D.
Wellwood (Mackie), Julie
Weston, Jane
Weston, John
Whitworth, P.
Wilson, Ian
Wilson, T.
Worral, Plum

APPENDIX 4

CAIRNGORM MOUNTAIN RESCUE TEAM
CALL-OUT LIST
June 1988

Police/Glenmore Lodge call the first available of: Peter Cliff, John Allen, Chris Barley, Dave Craig, Graham Clarke, Kenny Lindsay. That person calls the top name in each group, who is then responsible for calling the rest of his/her group.

		HOME				WORK		
Peter Cliff	Grantown	(	)	2824	or 3132 in emergency			
John Allen	Kingussie	(	)	244	Kingussie	(	)	202
Chris Barley	Aviemore	(	) 810505	Aviemore	(	)	301	
		or			Kingussie	(	)	280
Eric Pirie	Grantown	(	)	2395	Grantown	(	)	2395
Dr Peter Grant	Grantown	(	)	2196	Grantown	(	)	2484
Dr Leslie Cowan	Grantown	(	)	2484	Grantown	(	)	2484
Gordon Stewart	Grantown	(	)	3239	Grantown	(	)	2649
Paul Gray	Grantown	(	)	3349	Kingussie	(	)	350
Graham Clarke	Boat Garten	(	)	329	Boat Garten	(	)	329
Helen Geddes	Boat Garten	(	)	209	Boat Garten	(	)	209
Bill Marks	Dulnain Br.	(	)	302	Nairn	(	)	62274
Barney Mackie	Nethybridge	(	)	279	Nethybridge	(	)	279
Sarah Mather	Nethybridge	(	)	279	Nethybridge	(	)	279
Ann Wakeling	Aviemore	(	) 810818	Aviemore	(	) 811113		
John Gould	Aviemore	(	) 810337	Aviemore	(	) 810337		
Kenny Lindsay	Aviemore	(	) 810447	Aviemore	(	) 810222		
Stewart McNeish	Aviemore	(	) 810698	Kingussie	(	)	350	
Nick Forwood	Aviemore	(	) 810426	Aviemore	(	) 810729		
John Hall	Hopeman	(	) 830057	Hopeman	(	) 830863		
Richard Utton	Nairn	(	)	8413	Nairn	(	)	8413
Leslie MacDonald	Ballindall.	(	)	254	Aberlour	(	)	235
Moira/Dave Snadden	Kiltarlity	(	)	484	Beauly	(	) 782794	
Helen/Paul Ross	Inverness	(	) 232287	Inverness	(	) 232287		
Alex Sutherland	Gorthleck	(	)	641	Inverness	(	) 234121	
John Burns	Inverness	(	) 242509	Inverness	(	) 791965		
Malcolm Sclater	Inverness	(	) 238641	Inverness	(	) 239191		
Peter Finlayson	Inverness	(	) 241172	Inverness	(	) 234324		
Sarah Atkinson	Farr	(	)	312	Inverness	(	) 792424	
Donnie Williamson	Inverness	(	) 222232	Inverness	(	) 235241		
Ian McLean	Inverness	(	) 234109	Inverness	(	) 234131		
Chris Stuart	Inverness	(	) 225145	Inverness	(	) 221727		

Roger Gaff	Kincraig	(	)	245	Kincraig	(	)	265
Dave Craig	Kingussie	(	)	591	Kincraig	(	)	265
Ian Ross	Kingussie	(	)	392	Kincraig	(	)	265
Marjory Brown	Kincraig	(	)	265	Kincraig	(	)	265
Dick Arrowsmith	Kincraig	(	)	361	Kincraig	(	)	265
Alistair Cain	Kingussie	(	)	269	Cairngorm	(	)	261
Willie Todd	Kingussie	(	)	269	Kingussie	(	)	269
Dick Webster	Kingussie	(	)	484	Kingussie	(	)	475
Willie Anderson	Kingussie	(	)	779	Kingussie	(	)	475
John Lyall	Kincraig	(	)	221	Kincraig	(	)	223
Digby Bulmer	Newtonmore	(	)	402	Kincraig	(	)	223
Dave Morris	Newtonmore	(	)	466	Newtonmore	(	)	466
Wes Sterritt	Newtonmore	(	)	676	Cairngorm	(	)	261
Graeme Dalby	Newtonmore	(	)	542	Newtonmore	(	)	510
Bins Burley					Kingussie	(	)	350
Tim Duggleby	Spean Br.	(	)	510	Tulloch	(	)	245

Tel. Nos.:   Police: Aviemore (   ) 810222 and Inverness (   ) 239191
Achantoul Base: Aviemore (   ) 810477 (NCC), 810129 (MET)
Glenmore Lodge: Cairngorm (   ) 256